Paths to Transformation

Paths to Transformation

From Initiation to Liberation

○

KATE BURNS

CHIRON PUBLICATIONS

ASHEVILLE, NORTH CAROLINA

Book and cover design by Marianne Jankowski.
Printed in the United States of America.

Library of Congress Cataloging-in-Publication Data
Burns, Kate (Kathryn) (Jungian analyst)
  Paths to transformation : from initiation to liberation / Kate Burns.
     pages cm
Includes bibliographical references and index.
ISBN 978-1-63051-077-0 (pbk.) -- ISBN 978-1-63051-078-7 (hardback)
1. Jungian psychology. 2. Change (Psychology) 3. Self-realization. I. Title.

BF173.B882 2014
150.19'54--dc23

2013051251

CONTENTS

It is our nature to transform ourselves from time to time, whether or not we are ready for—or willing to—undergo such a process. The new must come at the expense of the old, and to cling to the old is to resist the fundamental law of nature: death before rebirth.

In *Paths to Transformation*, Jungian analyst Kate Burns brilliantly traces this process of death and rebirth that periodically occurs within each of us. Historically, the passage from adolescence to early adulthood was supported by extensive rites wherein wise elders, understanding the difficulty of moving from the dependency of childhood into adult responsibilities, invoked elaborate structures to propel the nascent psyche along developmental paths. To this end, such rites of passage tended to progress through six stages: separation from the hearth, metaphors to symbolize the death of childish ways, ceremonies of rebirth to facilitate the emergence of a new being, ancestral stories and practical skills to provide a sense of belonging as well as personal empowerment, ordeals whereby the youth might access inner resources for survival and adaptation, and finally reintegration into the community as a separated and empowered adult. We now know that the disappearance of such rites of passage have left modern youth adrift and dependent beyond their years, and more immature than at any time in human history.

Similarly, our ancestors venerated aging as a summons to wisdom. Aging was the fulfillment of nature, including its mortal goal, rather than a horror to be resisted through surgery and sundry denials. As a result, our contemporary flight from maturation and denial of death are perhaps our most neurotic symptoms, that is, where we are most thoroughly aligned against our nature.

Moreover, during the expanding years between youth and death, the question of how an individual is to separate from the blandishments and distractions of popular culture and find a personal path worthy of the soul remains almost wholly unaddressed. As more and more of us live longer, more and more are asking what the meaning of the second half of our lives might be. (In 1900, the average life span in North America was forty-seven; in 1934 it was sixty-three; today it is near ninety.) As this question becomes increasingly critical, there seem to be very few

resources available to help us find our way. Our culture offers material-
ism as an anodyne for undernourished souls; we have drugs to numb us
and a steady drumbeat of distractions to help us avoid reflecting on our
lives. Accordingly, addictions and eating disorders are more prevalent,
there are more types of depressions which resist medical treatment, and
so on. The contemporary collective psyche is in revolt everywhere; our
popular culture is a desperate contrivance to evade or anesthetize the
tocsin this insurgency from below offers each of us.

But run as we may, the psyche pursues and will not cease its symp-
tomatic summons to accountability. Among other founders of depth
psychology, Jung especially recognized the need to evolve a new "ritual,"
or set of attitudes and practices, to support the individual in finding an
authentic path through the thicket of postmodernism with its clamor-
ous voices and bramble of competing choices. While not everyone is in
therapy, everyone is, sooner or later, repeatedly invited by the psyche to
an accounting, to a dialogue, to a psycho-spiritual enlargement worthy
of the soul.

In *Paths to Transformation*, Burns clearly lays out the process through
which we all go, whether consciously or not. She does so without regard to whether or not one will emerge in the end larger and wiser. She
draws from her personal midlife struggle and the experience of working
through this transition with many patients. She integrates her scholarly
knowledge of anthropology, shamanism, tribal lore, alchemy, and other
ancient sources, and she delineates in a clear form the various stages
through which the process of death and rebirth passes.

In "Apprehending the Call" Burns notes how our symptoms—whether in our marriages, our bodies, our children, our troubled dreams—frequently signal us to consider the meaning of our journey. While we may
run from these invitations, drug them, anesthetize them, or suppress
them, they persist and intensify. Her description of how this call appears
has the potential to assist anyone toward a greater, more conscious recognition of the psyche's urgent summons.

In "Negotiating the Crisis" she illustrates from her life, from history,
from her patients, and from scholarly sources how people might better
undertake the internal dialogue asked of them. In "Living the Cure" she
is quite explicit about the changes that may be asked of us, the cost of
their denial, and what it really means to die in order that we may live in
a different way. In "Embodying Liberation" she describes how living in
a larger way is what nature asks of us, whether or not our changes and
transformations are understood and supported by others.

Paths to Transformation draws from life's sometimes painfully acquired personal understanding and provides concrete illustrations acquired from therapeutic practice. These are allied with a scholarly understanding of the resources of history and bring the reader to a deeper appreciation of the profound resources of our own nature. This includes the summons life brings to each of us to grow and a remembrance of the essential mystery that this journey we call our life really embodies. While thoroughly grounded in palpable research, this book is about real life, real people, real transformation happening within us all the time. Even more, it is a challenge to the reader to become more conscious and to undertake a more evolved partnership in the construction of our own lives.

James Hollis, PhD
Houston, Texas

INTRODUCTION

I was dead, then alive.
Weeping, then laughing.
The power of love came into me,
and I became fierce like a lion,
then tender like the evening star.

—RUMI

Insurgence

The wealth of material employing motifs of initiation seems daunting. In addition to a plethora of anthropological material, initiation permeates literary plots, personal stories, and profound encounters, all constellated by the insurgence of archetypal forces. However, my own experience and witnessing others in an analytical setting compels me to visit this kaleidoscopic archetype we all experience, not as a rite performed within the constructs of ancestral community but as an autonomous intrapsychic operation that creates the fates and stories of individuals and shapes their lives. Recognizing and engaging with initiation as an image of the psyche's propensity toward perpetual cycles of death and rebirth offers ever-expanding opportunities for emotional and spiritual healing.

The literature pertinent to the understanding of and in relation to initiatory practices and stories employs a span of inquiry which links science and art, religion and myth. Volumes of mystical theology from both East and West, philosophy, psychology, anthropology, poetry, literature and cinema, science fiction, even erotic literature, rightly belong in the field. Evidence of the archetype of initiation itself emerges, leaving the individual with creative and systematic ways to articulate the questions. We are left to follow Rilke's advice to the young poet: "*Live* the questions now" (1984, 34).

Consider a forty-year-old woman, recently married to a generous, loving, and reliable man who offers financial privilege and emotional stability. It seems to her that love has arrived on the wings of a dove.

Comfortable and cozy in her new life, she decides to explore a new area of study, one that has interested her most of her life. Almost ten years roll along while she immerses herself in fascination with the subject, which necessitates the discipline demanded by academic pursuit. One day she meets a man, seemingly unremarkable at first glance but also beguiling. She experiences an inexorable attraction that demands exploration and reflection. Her entire life comes into question, assuming telescopic clarity. She must change—or live a lie.

Does she remain in the marriage, or must she separate from it? Her decision seems to have implications for an entire world of individuals, including her world, and her relationship to it. However, only through dedicated self-reflection will she accomplish the mandated change. If she ignores the call and remains without change, she lives a lie. If she exits the marriage and leaps into another situation without articulating a meaningful narrative for the marriage, she will find herself in the same situation again: one that may appear superficially different but constellates the same old complexes in the same old way. When the question of what to do about a marriage enters into the analytical process, I usually begin by explaining that a satisfying explanation of one's position and involvement in the current alliance will lower significantly the chance of repetition of what seems like a situation that fails to nourish either party's growth.

Here I want to explain my definition of marriage. The foregoing example refers to a traditional marriage between man and woman. However, I enlist the word *marriage* to include any committed alliance between—or even among—individuals regardless of gender, license, or sanction by a religious group.

A quest for answers that will impart meaning to this conflict between inner imperative and outer limitation continually points toward some aspect of initiation. I seek to report on a varied and deeply emotional wandering. This requires a certain carving and shaping to create a loom on which to weave the serious inquirer into a variegated tapestry designed by the vibrant color of emotion rising out of intense experience and objective witnessing of oneself as initiate. My work will thus serve as both thread and loom. The threads issue from inner and outer personal experiences interwoven with cultural symbols of ritual, devotional systems, and myth. Jung's description of the flow of psychic energy held within foundational moments of initiation comprises the loom.

Initiation is triggered in various ways. Traumatic or unusual events, dreams and visions, or chronic illness often form an image in memory that later reveals itself further in the periodic calls to bring into consciousness those creative potentials buried among traumas of childhood. Initiation rites such as vision quests (once practiced to provide meaning and direction to a young person's interests and talents) now have been replaced by interest inventories, performance evaluations, and parental approval. In the first half of life, many are discouraged from interests fueled by enthusiasm in favor of endeavors fueled by desire for material benefits. In a social system ruled by one's ability to produce and to purchase, the activity of initiation proceeds from within the psyche rather than through outer rituals. These may reveal dangerous passages, frightening images, and traumatic dismembering in dreams and visions, synchronistic with challenging and sometimes devastating outer life events. When life seems mundane, boring, repetitive, and uninspiring, something happens that exacts a change. This change does not occur instantaneously but rather through the inception of a definable pattern practiced outwardly for millennia as initiation ritual. In our time, however, the numinous event, that is, an event permeated with mystery and meaning, whether an outer or inner experience, appears again as symbols in dreams and visions. This captures the attention of the individual and forces a return to the essential sphere of being around which one's incarnation took shape. When the nudge toward change is ignored, it may become a push, increasing in force until one feels shoved over the edge. Life-altering change that necessitates an initiation process typically follows a motif of descent.

Consider the following dream of the forty-year-old woman mentioned above:

I am in a very old and faded pickup truck that was once red. It is going along but seems to have no controls—no brakes, no steering wheel. I feel a bit uneasy, but it is going very slowly. Then the terrain becomes sloped and curvy. Now I am more concerned, searching for some kind of control mechanism. A sort of community is ahead, and I don't want to have a collision. Suddenly, a man is beside me who seems benevolent, kind, and seems to know me. I finally spot a small lever and slowly pull it toward me. The truck comes to a slow, safe stop. This settlement appears primal, with buildings made of dried mud. Then I am in one of the buildings, the man still with me. Inside the truck, I found an ancient toy that rattles, carved from a large dried gourd. For some reason I bring it with me. It has a feminine hourglass shape which reminds me of a primitive version of a Russian nested doll. It pulls apart back from front rather than top

from bottom. Inside I find a pair of dice. All the while, the man observes.
I feel a sense of mystery, like something ancient trying to communicate.

The forty-year-old woman was myself, introduced anonymously to illustrate the distance effected by the transformative events of initiation. The dream clusters with a number of others during the same time period which herald a particular readiness: a preparation within the psyche to reveal some unknown content of the unconscious that will change the outer attitude considerably. This particular dream anticipates a descent and a risk, motifs clearly inherent in initiation processes. The dream came at a time when outer life tumbled in turmoil, and everything was brought into question: a marriage outgrown and dissolving, a heart immersed in an ungrounded love affair, and the challenging vocational pursuit that precipitated its own initiatory pattern. The time seemed inappropriate for a descent that demanded sacred discernment in listening for what the ancient wisdom wanted to communicate. Psychologically, descent manifests as regression of psychic energy, a process described by Jung as mixing depression with anxiety.

At the time of this dream of descending to a place almost otherworldly in its simplicity, outer life demanded energy flowing out into preparation for studies, for nesting in single life, and for an emotionally perplexing love affair. Yet dream life suggested immanent descent, imaging the inward movement of psychic energy, a separation from imperatives and responsibilities of daily life, a descent imposed by autonomous forces. Such departure simply was not possible for her at the time. She must find a balance between inflowing psychic energy and the demands of daily life. The benevolent shamanic figure emanated reassurance. He looked like a middle-aged Bohemian poet with a twenties or thirties vintage short-brimmed hat, a loose, short-sleeved shirt, and khakis—not at all like a traditional tribal elder. He evoked a figure from the American Depression era, not nearly as long ago as suggested by the village of mud huts. Descent continues into some primal indigenous space below ground where the doll seems to have originated, somehow implanted with a pair of dice. The dice presented a curious image. What could they mean? My father was a gambler, but the throwing of the dice never held much interest for me. When discussing the dream with my analyst, he sat patiently waiting for me to dig within myself, not offering his characteristic flow of amplification. Finally I looked at him with an intense gaze and said, "I am a gambler of the heart." Therein I found a clue to the essence of myself. Later, the simple wisdom on a Yogi brand

tea bag came to mind: "Life is a chance, love is infinity, grace is reality."
Heart, intellect, and creature comforts all entered a state of flux. As it
turns out, the lover departed, creature comforts diminished to a mod-
estly embellished simplicity, and the enhanced intellect ebbs and flows.
A casual observer might say that I "bet the farm" and lost. Yet I did
not feel like a loser. I felt a trembling uncertainty, too daunting to view
fully, and knew that I must defer to something of my existence never
before known to me and perhaps imaged by the Bohemian companion.
Underworld dice suggest the certain presence of the insurgence of fate,
characterized by Jung as

> moments . . . when the universal laws . . . break in upon the purposes,
> expectations, and opinions of the personal consciousness, [and] are
> stations along the road of the individuation process. This process is,
> in effect, the spontaneous realization of the whole man. (Jung 1948b,
> par. 557)

These "stations along the road" of individuation comprise a cycle of
initiation, a symbolic death and rebirth that brings the personality one
realm closer to wholeness.

Whether from experiences engendered by fate or in response to impulses from within, both of which join synchronistically at some point,
countless insurgences of the soul's potentialities seek birth into one's life.
Given a readiness orchestrated by the intersection of inner spiritual and
emotional maturation and outer events, the ripe element pushes itself
into life with great force, often thrusting the individual into loss, emer-
gency, sacrifice, chaos, and pain, before the restored personality finds a
path of renewal.

Shortly after the dream, I stood perusing the selections at the Jung
Center bookstore and a compelling title caught my eye: Robert Ryan's
book *Shamanism and the Psychology of C. G. Jung.* In the book Ryan
draws intriguing parallels between visions reported by shamans that
occurred during their initiation ordeals and Jung's personal initiatory
experience. Ryan's comparison lent percipience to a number of dreams
of my own, as well as those of my clients which were suffused with
shamanic motifs. He gathered knowledge about shamanic initiation
rituals worldwide to exemplify the three phases of the process and then
drew comparisons with Jung's experience in midlife, when he created
the Red Book. Ryan's book provided much that amplified my process;
however, the question persisted, "Why now?" I was almost fifty years

old, well past the typical ages of adolescence and midlife (although contemporary society seems to agree that midlife now begins at fifty), when one theoretically hears a call into new pursuits. My devotion to Jungian psychology and the inception of my analysis had begun almost ten years before the dream, at the classic time of midlife. I wondered what message these dreams with decided initiatory motifs wanted to communicate. I wondered how the motifs of initiation could fit, but then I noticed that these three phases also follow Jung's formulation of the flow of psychic energy. Could the psyche enter into passage any time a ripe psychic content, like a seed ready to sprout, needed to issue forth, when an attitude needed to die so that a new one could emerge? Dyane Sherwood, in her contribution to a recent anthology, *Initiation: The Living Reality of an Archetype*, maintains that need for initiatory struggle presents itself at any time, and issues may arise from within as excruciating physical symptoms or dramatic imaginal experiences that seem somewhat impersonal. She also insists that death lurks in the initiatory pattern (2007, 103).

Observing dreams and synchronicities of patients, Jung noticed an ebb and flow of psychic energy, a continuous movement toward an un-predictable goal of greater awareness. An individual, through partici-patory experience in the vicissitudes of life and mobilizing the various qualities of character and awareness available to consciousness, attains a larger personality, a larger dialogue with life, truth, and spirit. When a person adopts an attitude of curiosity, relationship, and dialogue with the unique experiences that befall him or her, both within the imagina-tion and in the outer world, a maturation process ensues to which Jung assigned the term *individuation*.

This psychic interweaving of inner and outer significant experience which determines the uniqueness of each individual seems to mirror a phenomenon of the natural world that modern physics has described as chaos theory: unpredictable patterning. Physicists observe chaos by devising a relatively simple equation that involves raising the variable to a certain fractional power. An iterative process for deriving solutions to the equation requires that the output or solution becomes the input for the next iteration such that an ultimate solution does not exist. The infinite loop—bane of computer programmers—became a valuable tool of research into chaos theory. A plot of the results reveals bizarre and unpredictable patterns, yet patterns all the same. Not only do solutions to the equation generate unpredictable patterns, these patterns repeat themselves within themselves so that they appear the same under a microscope as they do viewed with the naked eye. A snowflake, for instance, while describing a finite shape cannot be measured in length; its length remains infinite. This phenomenon, in turn, finds description in the discipline of fractal geometry as self-similar patterns. In addition to the snowflake, fractal geometry explains, for example, the phenomenon of a leaf becoming a recognizable variety of leaf as the inner vein structure forms repetitive self-similar images. Small changes in the initial conditions of fractal equations can produce strikingly different results. Each and every leaf remains unique and unpredictable.

Jung's observations of the unfolding of the individuation process mirrors these phenomena observable in nature so that the becoming of a human being throughout life proceeds with the same pattern as the smaller episodes of individuation we call initiation. One could say that the iterations of initiatory episodes within a person's life are self-similar. The lifelong process of individuation not only proceeds according to iterative repetition of a number of subprocesses, these processes follow a pattern resembling traditional initiation tasks that have been performed since the dawn of human consciousness. Each subprocess enacts a ritual procedure which among modern people originates within the psyche and brings an important potential aspect of one's personality into awareness with each successful completion. The output then becomes the input for the next episode, and growth occurs each time so that one's personality experiences growth in perspective and awareness of inner as well as outer life. The individual, while occupying a finite space, reveals infinite and unpredictable facets of personality.

Ebb and flow of psychic energy follows a pattern. Authors by and large describe patterns of initiation in a three-step process, adopting terms fitting to the particular initiatory environment. Robert Ryan (2002) appropriates the terms *call, crisis, cure* to describe shamanic initiation; author Joseph Campbell (1949/1968) describes the hero's journey as *departure, trials and victories, return*; Jungian analyst Murray Stein (1983), describing the midlife initiatory psychic crisis, enlists the terms *separation, liminality, reintegration*; Edith Turner (1996) summarizes ritual procedure with *separation, transition, reassimilation*; and Mircea Eliade explains:

> the fundamental pattern of all initiations: first, torture at the hands of
> demons or spirits, who play the role of masters of initiation; second,

xvii

ritual death, experienced by the patient as a descent to Hell or an ascent to Heaven; third, resurrection to a new mode of being—the mode of 'consecrated man,' that is, a man who can personally communicate with gods, demons, and spirits. (1958, 91)

I have found, however, that a description of the flow of psychic energy as observed and reported by Jung, even though initiatory in character, requires a few substeps in order to more fully communicate the variety of experience involved. Seven phases more clearly articulate the psychic process:

1. An intrapsychic conflict develops.
2. The individual is challenged to contain the tension.
3. A regression of psychic energy ensues, attracted by the tension.
4. Unconscious images are activated by the influx of energy.
5. A reconciling symbol emerges out of the images, providing the individual with a sense of meaning and purpose.
6. Progression of psychic energy canalizes into new activities.
7. A transcendent function of consciousness brings to the individual renewed ways of being and interacting in the world.

Each step of initiation offers spiritual confrontation, struggle, support, and, potentially, subsequent healing. In the chapters that follow, I present a pattern of initiation that superimposes the fundamental three-phase traditional process—that is, call, crisis, and cure—onto a seven-step psychological flow of psychic energy through which modern culture meets its ancestors and abstract psychological experience finds meaning in myth and religion.

Shamanic initiation practices bring color and dance and song to Jung's abstract concept of individuation and the flow of psychic energy, out of which a living symbol may emerge. An initiating shaman must follow the searching self into the underworld and join with the stench of death lurking there, then tear to pieces every preconceived notion that undermines the sacred call of an individual life, while watching and experiencing the terror of his or her own dismemberment, disembowelment, or skinning, until the symbol emerges that will re-member the soul body and liberate the tormented initiate from inner suffering.

While reading about the decidedly traumatic experiences and visions of initiating shamans all over the world I had a dream like no other I could remember. It left me confused and somewhat frightened.

*I am kneeling over my own dead body which is lying in yogic Shivasana,
or "dead body pose." My kneeling body feels somewhat ethereal.*

In my practice I have noticed that every time a client dreams of a death
of the dream ego, I get the question, "Am I going to die?" Likewise
when I awakened from the dream I thought, "Might this mean I am
going to die?" even though my experience in training assured me that
most likely the death I had witnessed in the dream meant a symbolic
death. I decided to explore the image more deeply. The goal of *Shivasana*—to lie completely still, not even moving an eyelid, and with im-
perceptible breath—often challenges Western people more than any
other yoga asana, or posture. Named after Shiva, god of death and
rebirth, this posture serves to rejuvenate the body after challenging
practice involving flexibility, strength, balance, and endurance, which
makes *Shivasana* the most important posture. Heinrich Zimmer, a
foremost authority on Indian culture, explains Shiva as "the embodiment of Super-Death . . . dissolving all things, all beings, all divinities,
in the crystal pure, . . . But then again as Shishu, the babe, the crescent
moon . . . a promise of life and life-strength" (1946, 167). The dream
anticipates in one numinous image the objective and goal of initiation:
breakdown (through strenuous and challenging evaluation of social
constructs) of family patterns and traditions and outworn forms of
expression (body), thus setting the stage for the emergence of a new
form of expression.

Just as big dreams often will, this brief image kept revealing itself. Over
a year later, preparing to teach a class in lucid dreaming, I read in Carlos
Castaneda's *The Art of Dreaming*: "The third [and final] gate of dreaming
is reached when you find yourself in a dream, staring at someone else
who is asleep. And that someone else turns out to be you" (1993, 141).
Had I achieved the gift, the final gate, without attempting the first two?
Rather than a gift, however, the dream anticipated a crisis that would
leave me shaken and disoriented, a ghostlike wanderer with only the
pattern and ancient symbols of initiation to offer meaning and motivation in continuing my work. These myths instilled "a promise of life and
life-strength," while feelings of confusion and disorientation plagued
my experience (Zimmer 1946, 167). I wandered almost aimlessly in the
middle phase of the initiation process, described by Stein as *liminality*,
whereby "the sense of 'I-ness' and some of its continuities remain . . .
[while] the prevailing feeling is one of alienation, marginality, and
drift" (1983, 9).

Full-blown crisis followed over a year later on the heels of another quite disturbing dream:

> I am about to be executed. I have committed a crime against the state; but it was necessary for the revolutionary cause. A man is with me who has also been caught. We are preparing to lie down on a kind of operating table because we are going to be skinned alive.

An ominous foreboding upon waking from the dream proved appropriate. Less than two weeks later the relationship that had entangled me in a web of erotic fantasy, passionate love, and inspiration ended rather abruptly, leaving me in a state of emotional shock. Over the next two years I found myself inexorably drawn into what felt like a life and death struggle to gather my heart; expressed psychologically, to honor the symbol and allow it to guide me into new life. Here lies the crux of such a passage, namely, that one acknowledges a transcendent function of consciousness. Images of the hero's return to the tribe illustrate this last, seventh phase. The returning hero has become a person whom the community no longer knows or understands. This individual has withstood annihilation at the hands of demonic spirits and has emerged as someone able to communicate with higher consciousness in an effort to guide others into healing. While I have experienced this process as my story, I have found within it a timeless, universal story. We "dream the myth onwards" by apprehending and conveying the archetypal energies that carry us onward, whether we wish to or not (Jung 1951, par. 271).

Assumptions

The ideas in this book rest on discoveries I've encountered about my own nature, perspectives, and values, which form a pillar of assumptions. While not in the scope of this work to argue my positions formally, stating them may reassure the reader that I have considered my platform and carved a foundational support for the symbolic process herein described.

I embrace the idea that an essence exists within the individual psyche, as well as in any system of thought or religious teaching or culture itself, that harbors abiding truth no matter how completely the winds of change alter outworn tenets of outer expressions. Jung thought of the Self as an essence of the psyche, the center and circumference of the individual. I am also convinced of the existence of archetypes, of ideas both psychological and cultural that exist independently and that influence thought, art, and civilization. Moreover, I embrace archetypal power, both instinctual and spiritual, as the Real: an ineffable force which predetermines, transcends, resides with, and influences the material world, bridging the gap of unconsciousness between spirit and matter. This assumption is currently attracting a wealth of controversy among scholars of Jungian theory. My own position, while decidedly polarized, concurs with my observations, both cultural and clinical. Jung exerted great effort to establish evidence for the influence of archetypes on psyche and matter; my observations support his assertions. I believe this issue, while complicated and unprovable, demands decision on my part given my responsibility to those who seek my counsel.

I am a romanticist by nature, in the classical sense that love and beauty are divine attributes and tragedy reveals beauty. In my experience mysticism overrides dogma, and metaphysics provides for the mystery that lures the individual into creative exploration and expression. I find initiation meaningful in that it allows one to reflect on life and self and to experience as well as form a connection to that essence which insists on perpetual creativity, allowing one to awaken beauty.

1

Apprehending the Call

*The call is the directive which, in calling to and calling upon,
in reaching out and inviting, directs us toward an action or
non-action, or toward something even more essential. In
every calling, a call has already gathered. The calling is not a
call that has gone by, but one that has gone out and as such is
still calling and inviting; it calls even if it makes no sound.*
—MARTIN HEIDEGGER, *WHAT IS CALLED THINKING?*

*There is no change that is unconditionally valid over a
long period of time. Life has always to be tackled anew.*
—C. G. JUNG, "THE TRANSCENDENT FUNCTION"

Of the seven steps in the flow of psychic energy outlined in the introduction (p. xviii), intimations of *call* flow through the first two: (1) conflict, and (2) containing the tension. A conflict, at first unnoticed by
consciousness, forms in the hinterlands of the unconscious. One experiences vague symptoms, feelings of restlessness. A paramount challenge
ensues, demanding that the client or initiate maintain a certain compo-
sure until this restlessness relaxes into an inner silence so that the sound
of the call may find clear reception.

Initiation cycles may interrupt life when one's situation seems quite
all right, even if daily experience rests in a medium wanting vitality.
Mircea Eliade, a leading scholar of traditional initiation rites, describes
the process as "a break with the universe of daily life" (1958, 101).

In our society of cell phones, email, inexhaustible amounts of information, and perpetually demanding responsibilities, breaking with
daily life poses the greatest challenge. A typical individual with family,
career, and financial obligations, together with personal goals, desires,
and interests, shudders to entertain even the thought of separating for

a while by perhaps turning off all communication devices and strolling in silence among nature, listening to the symphonies of birdsong at dawn and insects at dusk. Yet, when the soul calls one into just such a retreat, it may be a matter of life and death.

Call may conceal itself in two main circumstances of life, each typically attracting an opposite feeling response. Call to a larger existence may enter one's life embedded in loss or in opportunity; loss brings grief, opportunity beckons as desire or inspiration. Whichever arrives first, the other will soon follow, and then one has entered the precincts of initiation.

The vignette of the forty-year-old woman portrayed in the introduction exemplifies initiation provoked by an erotic encounter that seems to arrive out of nowhere. However, a number of fateful circumstances may thrust one into the throes of an initiation cycle:

1. One may lose an employment situation that defines identity and insures financial well-being. Whether one parts with an employer according to one's own volition or due to the employer's circumstances, and no matter at what time of life, including retirement, a period of self-assessment ensues which creates a transitional time of wandering through a field of possibility. A sense of terror, uncertainty, and/ or insecurity, concern for loved ones, self-doubt, and sometimes self-recrimination, will permeate the situation.

2. Certain individuals experience a dream or vision that unravels their entire religious position and sends them on a quest for a deeper formulation of the meaning of existence itself, in particular, the meaning of their own existence.

3. An undeveloped or only partially developed talent may capture one's attention, demanding time, energy, and focus currently usurped by life's responsibilities and necessities. Often these talents suffered in the shadows due to prevailing family or cultural value systems, which in turn the individual must confront, reassess, and perhaps repudiate.

4. A sudden illness may change one's relationship with life of and within the body.

5. A loved one may die, leaving an empty space in the heart that compels the survivor to build an altar and, in so doing, find a different relationship to that loved one as well as to all other relationships prescient in one's life.

Resistance to these calls manifests in chronic depression, addiction, self-mutilation, stress-related illness, even death. Questions arise out of the intensity of an insistence of inner potential to find an avenue of expression in the world countered by an outer life already saturated with duties, details, and obligations.

Answering the call means beginning to prepare for something vague at best and totally unknown at worst. It means finding space, clearing space, or creating space, and attention to the smallest or most undervalued thing. It means loading the vessel of outer life with only the necessities, discerning between the necessary and the superfluous. In the words of Mircea Eliade, it means "a break with the universe of daily life" (1958, 101). It is a separation from the mundane—sanctification. Like a shape-shifter, a call arrives in many guises, in a score of voices, and at unpredictable intervals throughout life's journey. We have a choice whether or not to follow, but meaningless suffering continually threatens to extinguish the soul before the body even slows.

The very first whispers of a call may feel like pursuit by unseen forces, an inexplicable dissonance or inner disturbance; dreams appear that don't seem to speak to the life one currently lives. When ignored, these feelings manifest as insoluble conflicts, both in dream images and in outer reality. Ignoring the conflict often leads to depression or accidents. It may also appear as an illness that harnesses one into a more introspective situation where the command to contain the tension invites itself, like the thirteenth fairy at the christening of Aurora in "Sleeping Beauty."

Conflict

Call implies a following, a choice, even if all avenues forward seem fraught with difficulty and sacrifice. The conflict as to whether or not one chooses to embrace the great unknown arrives in concert with an inner imperative that holds one's feet to the flame, demanding devotion. One person will want to follow the inspiration but will see no way, no clear path. Another person will resist with every sinew of strength available. Both will often find themselves putting a toe in the water, placing one foot on the path, and amazingly enough, some energy is set in motion that begins to clear the path or part the waters.

According to testimonies of practicing shamans, choice is an illusion. Curiously enough, they find solace in the possibility that an agonizing, even potentially fatal, initiatory experience may position them to find meaning embedded in the torturous visions and paralyzing illnesses. Rolling Thunder, a Native American medicine man, characterized his own spiritual calling as "a power which comes to you, which you have to honor, respect, and use, otherwise it can make you sick" (Ryan 2002, 92). Ryan reports that certain tribes even force a young man to undergo shamanic initiation against his will if he has a history of suffering those symptoms believed to indicate potential healing powers:

> throughout the whole continent [of South America] "the potential medicine man is suddenly struck by a call from the spirits; in many places they handle him roughly and among the Araucanians he is forced to accept the office against his will." (2002, 91–92)

Amid spiritual crisis, young members of the tribe are sacrificed to an initiatory process that exacts a terrifying passage accompanied by abject aloneness further exacerbated by symbolic death. Some initiates do not survive. Resistance to their call, however, creates inner turmoil, a spiritual crisis. Eliade asserts:

> the shamanic vocation often implies a crisis so deep that it sometimes borders on madness. And since the youth cannot become a shaman until he has resolved this crisis, it is clear that it plays the role of a *mystical initiation*. . . . The disorder provoked in the future shaman by the agonizing news that he has been chosen by the gods or the spirits is by that very fact valuated as an initiatory sickness. The precariousness of life, the solitude and the suffering, that are revealed by any sickness are, in this particular case, aggravated by he symbolism of initiatory death; for accepting the supernatural election to the divine or demonic powers, hence that one is destined to immanent death. (1958, 89)

Absence of formal initiatory ritual in current Western culture has forced the archetype of initiation into the unconscious where it remains undeveloped and most often seeks expression in violent acts of self-destruction. Even in the face of call or crisis, initiation may fail and cure may remain elusive such that consciousness remains constricted. Substance abuse, for instance, creates an unfulfilled initiation with repetitions that prevent individuals from ever bringing embodiment to the insistent creative yearnings of their souls. Suicide, a desire for instantaneous transformation, derails initiation, a case enacted when ego consciousness perceives very limited avenues of expression and thereby concretizes the urge of the inner self to symbolically kill off an outworn ego attitude so that a new life may emerge. Why does the incidence of suicide increase among adolescents? Young people in Western society struggle under a system that offers few opportunities for mentoring and unique self-expression while exerting enormous pressure to compete, to excel, and to become a source of esteem for parents who have little self-esteem.

Imagine a person trying to negotiate the challenges of the teen years, but who periodically receives strange visions or disturbing dreams. Knowing that accessible authority figures would most likely diminish these experiences as "just" the imagination or would overreact to them with mandatory medication, hospitalization, or both, the youth remains silent. Perceived inability to "fit in" prompts feelings of worthlessness and hopelessness sustained by fear. This person discovers that getting high or drunk with friends provides an escape from these powerful feelings. Addiction or suicide, whether accidental or intentional, ensues. Such a scenario, unfortunately, occurs much more often than most people want to admit. Tragically, lives could often be saved by simple attention to a young person's inner striving and by offering guidance that opens the field of possibilities for available forms of expression.

For a modern person at any age, the task of initiation proceeds intra-psychically, often commencing with a seemingly benign vague feeling that life has lost something, that the activities and amusements that once brought a feeling of excited anticipation have lost their luster. Or perhaps something new appears in one's life that awakens the senses and brings a spring to the step, yet some taboo prevents immediate embrace. A feeling of guilt may lurk beneath the welter or turmoil of emotion inherent in the challenges of entry into an endeavor to change. One may ask, "Now what kind of self-aggrandizing inflation could take me away from my responsibilities to spouse and family, not to mention the other sacrifices they may encounter?" Often the whole thrust toward a renewed perspective ends with such a question. Yet certain individuals continue on, almost hypnotized by the luster of restored hope, with no idea how or if the task will be accomplished. Perhaps the money will run out; perhaps the stress inherent in the situation will interrupt the process with an illness. Nothing makes sense. Equally senseless, the force that keeps one moving forward toward a loosely defined goal often arrives as a comforting feeling, as if a spirit presence has arrived in the middle of the night and whispered to you that everything will be all right. Something inside shifts, and the decision to go forward in faith fashions a heartfelt certainty that this creative madness will find its way and its clarity. Jung positions vocation in the realm of divine law:

> True personality is always a vocation and puts its trust in it as in God, despite its being, as the ordinary man would say, only a personal feeling. But vocation acts like a law of God from which there is no escape. The fact that many a man who goes his own way ends in ruin means nothing to one who has a vocation. He *must* obey his own law, as if it were a daemon whispering to him of new and wonderful paths. Anyone with a vocation hears the voice of the inner man: he is *called*. (1934c, par. 300)

Whether experienced as inner turmoil or outer temptation, one enters the realm of call and must make the difficult choice whether to engage in the process of psychic renewal involving symbolic death that tortures the soul or suffer the consequences of refusing a natural process of growth even though it could turn in on itself and show up in a life-threatening illness or life-negating neurosis, even psychosis. When a client enters my office for the first time I usually get some picture of the situation that catapulted the individual to what is often the last resort: therapy with a stranger. Some life-altering decision that cannot find a solution or a loss ungrieved and unresolved has brought this individual to unbearable agony.

Shamanic initiation presupposes suffering, imaged in visions and dreams of agonizing dismemberment and death which, in turn, result in the ability to apprehend and supplicate transcendent beings believed to possess powers of healing. Due to the neophyte's courage and creativity in surviving such trauma, subsequently healing himself or herself, the tribe ascribes these healing powers to the initiated shaman, hence, *wounded healer*. Jung notes,

> the "making of a medicine-man" involves, in many parts of the world, so much agony of body and soul that permanent psychic injuries may result. His "approximation to the savior" is an obvious consequence of this, in confirmation of the mythological truth that the wounded wounder is the agent of healing, and that the sufferer takes away suffering. (1954b, par. 457)

Initiatory death, described as symbolic, does not mean less agony than actual death. During the throes of my own tortured grief, my analyst, seemingly imparting some transcendent announcement, said to me, "A suffering soul is worse than a suffering body." It sounded remotely absurd, but I knew he was right.

Rites of initiation have evolved with respect to a number of developmental transitions and spiritual traditions that share certain motifs; however, I wish herein to consider the culture and images of shamanic systems of symbols in an attempt to amplify the archetypal patterning that expresses itself in the motif of the wounded healer. Psychologically considered, this means an intrapsychic potential is revealed through embracing a willingness to live the meaning inherent in one's existence, to redeem the myth perhaps lost within some wound reaching as far back as early childhood or beyond.

By "redeem the myth," I mean a process of discovering a story, foundational to one's existence, that has been lost in the process of becoming conscious. It is a process whereby attitudes and value systems of the family, society, and culture influence awareness, and one fashions oneself in accordance with those values and attitudes. One learns the laws of the world and embraces ambitions important to one's material livelihood. The degree of orderliness of one's outer experiences during this developmental phase of learning carries immeasurable importance because it may have a critical influence on the strength of character necessary to confront and evaluate learned patterns of thinking and behavior effectively as an individual matures. A person who experiences too much chaos and lack of integrity in caregivers and community leaders faces a great danger of becoming tangled up in wounds of outer circumstances and may never turn attention inward to find the individual story or myth. Discovering the forgotten story depends upon attending to the life of the unconscious through dreams and imagination, going inward to discern the tale that enacts a parallel life, without which one lives less than half an existence.

The following story had not been forgotten by any means; however, its archetypal significance in the life of the child had been reduced to mere coincidence.

It was that time of day we call dusk. The Irish and Celts call it a "thin time": between light and dark, after the sun has dropped below the horizon but still washes the sky with shimmering light that seems alive with faerie folk and leprechauns and other beings of the world beyond. Her father, whom she called "Daddy," was trimming the bushes recently plant-

ed in the front yard while the little four-year-old girl watched, fascinated by whatever this curious and furtive individual chose to do. The sun continued to set, and just before darkness swallowed this fateful day her father gently instructed her to get into the house. Walking across the front yard with a lack of vigilance inherent in her protected life, she stepped too close to a Texas copperhead, extremely poisonous, potentially lethal. Her screams announced the sudden injection, the pain and fright that filled her little body, small for her age. She held her ankle for her mother to inspect just as her father leapt into the house behind her. Two bloody holes revealed an unmistakable diagnosis, and in seconds the young family— father, pregnant mother, two-year-old brother, and bitten sister—were racing toward the local clinic.

A split second of fate in mid-September changed this little girl's life forever. Four months later, the dawning of the new year found her in a hospital bed suffering from Gillian-Barre syndrome, a neurological disease that affects the nerve myelin and results in numbness of the limbs. Only a few cases had been documented at the time, and the medical establishment dismissed any cause and effect relationship between snake and disease. The child's soul, however, joined them indelibly so that they sit together at the center of memory, perpetually informing both outer and inner life. One could say that in the world of the soul everything occurs in present tense. Jung, in his extensive studies of mythological motifs, noticed a simultaneity or eternal process whereby significant events continue to express themselves infinitely (1952a, par. 629). Events that impress a child as something mythic are the rule rather than the exception.

When I entered analysis roughly forty years later and commenced a practice of faithfully writing down my dreams and considering the meanings of their images, I realized that the part of myself who was the bitten little girl longed for the opportunity to share her serpent-mediated wisdom. Snakes populated my dreams as if, according to their nature, the cold-blooded creatures had hibernated deep in my psyche. Serpents of every size and color imaginable entered my dreams. In addition to copperheads, I encountered rattlesnakes, cobras, pythons, boas, giant snakes of mythic proportions, tiny snakes newly hatched, exotic brightly colored snakes, water snakes, and desert snakes. At first these slithery reptiles would capture me into paralyzed attention, threatening the slightest move. But eventually certain ones felt numinous in a different way. They invited connection and communication, even benevolence.

In temples of Asclepius, nonvenomous snakes crawled around the floor in honor of the god who was thought to have received secret knowledge from a snake which licked his ears clean.[1] Indigenous cultures of the Americas continue to conduct snake ceremonies in their initiation rituals, and shamanic initiation and ceremonial practices often involve deadly snakes. One bitten who lives may receive the snake as their totem animal, a spiritual ally or guide. Initiates not bitten have also endured and accomplished the initiatory trial. Those chosen by the snake are believed to have received an ability to transmute poisons, whether physical or spiritual.

Among the Hopi, kivas scattered throughout the deserts of New Mexico and Arizona serve as initiation sites for a number of ceremonies involving poisonous snakes. Initiation in the kiva often means encounter with one or more of these deadly creatures. An initiate's power then rests in whether or not the serpent decides to bite and whether the venom proves deadly. On the last evening of a four-day period during which initiates gather snakes for the Hopi snake-antelope ceremony, the captured creatures are blessed. Chiefs and initiates sit in a circle singing soft and low while as many as sixty snakes roam freely around the kiva. Old chiefs may attract a number of snakes, which curl up and sleep on their laps during the ceremony. It is believed that the snakes can discern a pure heart and a peaceful mind (Waters 1963, 221). Among the Wiradjuri of Australia initiates receive magical powers by snakes rubbing themselves against the initiates' bodies (Eliade 1964, 135).

These examples set the ancestral stage of the collective unconscious for a recurrent expression of a split-second event in the psyche of an ordinary little girl. Each of you has experienced something during childhood that made a deep impression on your subsequent life and on your soul. It seems often the case with analysands that the most significant event of childhood comes tumbling into the conversation after many sessions, sometimes over several years. I never mentioned the experience of my own snakebite to my analyst until I had a dream of snakes and she wanted to know my associations. Why had I, and later my analysts, not thought of this pivotal moment of childhood before? Such an event reveals an enormous key that unlocks so many of the riddles of our lives and brings to light so many fearful corners. Perhaps it's one of those swept-under-the-carpet events, never mentioned, but permeated with feelings of shame or deep terror that rob the child of the value of its own experience. My family considered the bite simply one of those happenstances of life that occasionally makes a good story. How amazing that only a hundred years before, in America, the indigenous culture struggling to preserve its myths and its wisdom, would have venerated a child who survived a poisonous snakebite. Of course, I did not survive on my own, but at the hands of Western medicine. However, just as easily the medicine could have failed in some way. Mystery always permeates survival of a life-threatening trial.

More than fifty years later, a female shaman in Zurich gifted with seeing past lives perceived one of my past lives in a hidden cottage where I was raised by a man gifted in the occult arts—she called him an alchemist. According to her, I had been orphaned when my mother was burned at the stake for practicing witchcraft. During that life I had been too frightened to practice the healing art taught to me by my foster father. I accepted this provocative image offered by the shaman in honor of the unconscious just as I would honor one of my own dreams, and I could not help asking myself if I am not now living the life I had forgotten, that past life still longing to be lived. Certainly the image infuses my own strivings with a meaning permeated with energy. Was this forgotten image secretly piloting my irrational impulse to study analytical psychology? What might have happened to me if I had not mustered the courage? I can imagine some of the possibilities: anxiety attacks, depression, compulsive and destructive behavior, death. I am no stranger to any of those sufferings except physical death; however, the meaning inherent in my vocation continues to lift me out of the throes of fear and sadness and remains the wellspring of my life.

The ego during initiatory experiences must simultaneously submit and endure. Then, between the serpent seeking your heart and your sweating brow, the lion or tiger roars your new name, that is, an instinctual power anticipates a new personality long before ego consciousness even receives a mandate for change, a call. Jungian analyst and author James Hollis asserts this reality:

> The astonishing fact is that when we suffer from inner, as opposed to outer, sources, our psyche is registering a huge fact, a life transforming fact, if we can surrender to it, namely: the psyche has a better plan for our lives than our ego's plan, or our culture's plan. This sounds simple enough, even reasonable, but no ego consciousness is thrilled at overthrow, critique, or humbling. Yet from this bewildering deconstruction, the real project our lives embody can emerge, and be rendered palpable, which always requires of us, despite our desires for comfort and predictability, a change of and an enlargement of consciousness. (2009, 151)

Not everyone who endures a process of initiation, or enlargement of personality, will express their new attitude in the realm of healing per se. The process presupposes endurance of great challenges which endow the individual with a newfound feeling of personal power and insight that expresses itself in creative ways as varied as the individuals who emerge. I am reminded of a story Jung recounted as an example of "being in Tao," told to him by Richard Wilhelm:

> There was a great drought where Wilhelm lived; for months there had not been a drop of rain and the situation became catastrophic.... Finally the Chinese said, "We will fetch the rain-maker." And from another province a dried up old man appeared. The only thing he asked for was a quiet little house somewhere, and there he locked himself in for three days. On the fourth day the clouds gathered and there was a great snow-storm at the time of the year when no snow was expected, an unusual amount, and the town was so full of rumours about the wonderful rain-maker that Wilhelm went to ask the man how he did it.... And the little Chinese said: "I did not make the snow, I am not responsible.... I come from another country where things are in order. Here they are out of order, they are not as they should be by the ordinance of heaven. There the whole country is not in Tao, and I also am not in the natural order of things because I am in a disordered country. So I had to wait three days until I was back in Tao and then naturally the rain came." (1955–56, par. 604n)

The initiate steps into Tao at the moment the call sings out above the clutter and noise of daily life and receives an answer composed of devotion carving a protective niche into the matrix of meaninglessness. Enduring the torture and suffering of a liminal state where all assumptions stand in the balance and nothing seems sure paradoxically brings one into order from within. Does this inner order affect the outer order of things? Does one have a responsibility to answer the call of the soul, allowing it to permeate one's activities? Such an irrational idea seems ridiculous to a modern scientific mind; however, devotees of wisdom traditions and mystics for thousands of years have practiced meditation, prayers, yoga, and rituals with just this idea in mind. Ochwiay Biano (Mountain Lake), chief of the Taos Pueblos, told Jung,

> "What we do, ... we do it for the whole world." ... "You think, then, that what you do in your religion benefits the whole world?" He replied with

great animation, "Of course. If we did not do it, what would become of the world?" And with a significant gesture he pointed to the sun.

. . . "After all," he said, "we are a people who live on the roof of the world; we are the sons of Father Sun, and with our religion we daily help our father to go across the sky. We do this not only for ourselves, but for the whole world. If we were to cease practicing our religion, in ten years the sun would no longer rise. Then it would be night forever." (1961, 252)

Biologists in virtually every persuasion share the opinion that planet Earth appears bound for a major crisis due, for the most part, to its human population's disregard for the delicate interdependence of ecosystems. Could the individual, by renewing a meaningful connection to soul, serve to usher the planet through such a crisis? In noticing how indigenous Americans had found a cosmological meaning for their lives, Jung realized that the great stores of knowledge amassed through civilization had estranged its people from nature and the mythic world and corrupted the vitality inherent in grasping a meaning for their lives (ibid.).

Call very often is embodied as the core of loss, when one feels gripped by deep feelings of abandonment, isolation, rejection, and powerlessness; in short, tortured grief, whereby one's very soul seems unhinged or, conversely, constricted. Symptoms in modern psychological language include depression, anxiety, or feelings of guilt and shame, the latter issuing from value systems that fail to appropriate space for discomfort due to emotional disturbances. One feels an absence of motivation toward routine tasks, a depletion of forward thrust, of the energy that fuels one into the day; the agenda has deteriorated. Like an exhausted field no longer able to nourish a crop, one must lie fallow for a while, allow nutrients to gather, and then often must nourish a quite different crop.

Here, in keeping with the shamanic experience, it is important to make a distinction between pathological diagnoses and initiatory suffering. Terms like *depression* and *anxiety* communicate in modern language what Jung describes as evidence of "disalliance with the unconscious . . . synonymous with loss of instinct and rootlessness" (1943, par. 195). The situation becomes potentially pathological only when the psychic imperative inherent in such experience goes unattended. Jung noticed that when consciousness becomes immersed in a one-sided relationship with life so that inner images receive no attention, psychic breakdown occurs which announces itself in declining instinct, trepidation, disorientation, and involvement in messy circumstances that cannot be solved (1957, par. 15).

Ryan reports similar symptoms gathered from shamans asked to remember their experiences as members of the community. They describe a meditative attitude, with a propensity for seeking solitude, sleeping a great deal, absent-mindedness, prophetic dreams, and torture in the throes of unpredictable seizures (Ryan 2002, 97). A young person exhibiting such symptoms today might receive a diagnosis of clinically depressed or the most common one among young people, attention deficit hyperactivity disorder (ADHD), along with a prescription for the newest generation of psychopharmaceuticals.

Sir Ken Robinson, a world-renowned thinker on creativity, education, and human potential, questions whether ADHD actually exists and asserts definitively that the proportions of ADHD diagnosis constitute a "fictitious epidemic." He notices that incidence of the disorder has risen in proportion to the rise in standardized testing. Creativity, a process of discovering original and valuable ideas, according to Robinson, requires "divergent thinking" which involves an ability to realize a variety of interpretations of a given question as well as numerous answers. Medications interrupt the natural creative process by anaesthetizing a child's experience, that is, reversing the aesthetic experience of being fully alive and present in the current moment. Robinson invites us to examine our motives for education and for development of the process of thinking as our societies, both East and West, enter the twenty-first century. I wonder if we have something to learn from communities not integrated into our cause-and-effect, linear-thinking society.[2]

By participating directly in their environment, indigenous cultures enjoy a vitality which puts them in direct connection with what Sir Robinson refers to as aesthetic experience, a prerequisite to creativity. During his first journey to Africa, Jung noticed that the indigenous communities he met expressed an effervescence of spirit, a vitality rooted in *participation mystique*, which he likened to a harmonious interplay between conscious thinking and the unconscious, or soul. While he valued his own erudite mind, he longed for the joie de vivre uninterrupted among the communities of Africa. Western culture (which includes much of the East due to enculturation) faces the problem of healing the split ruptured between consciousness and soul due to overdeveloped valuing of conscious linear thought. If any answers lie buried in age-old shamanic practices, we might consider the importance of ceremony and ritual and contents of the unconscious such as dreams and visions.

13

Could the spectacular rise in the incidence of ADHD diagnoses indicate an entire generation captured by the soul's longing to receive some attention?

Mircea Eliade articulates a careful distinction between psychopathology and shamanic vocation, emphasizing the initiatory structure and experience of meaning which replicates a mystical pattern and often brings the future shaman to experience a disintegration of the personality resembling psychosis. However, Eliade describes the madness as initiatory death which enacts an experience of "precosmogonic" chaos, with the intention of preparing a new creation. The profane man, or misguided ego consciousness, must dissolve so that a new personality can emerge (Eliade 1958, 89). A state of crisis and chaos, within and often synchronistically evident in outer life for modern people, continues until one turns attention inward, imaginally enters initiatory space, and observes messages that may seem to make little sense when exposed to linear thinking. Psychologically, for children, ADHD represents the frustration of unguided attempts to turn attention inward. For adults the frustration emerges as anxiety attacks, depression, bipolar episodes, and adult incidences of ADHD.

Not always does call follow on the heels of loss beyond one's control. Rather than wrestling with choices inherent in answering a call to prepare for the creation of a new personality, one may feel abducted like a young and naïve Persephone. In this case initiation steals in like a thief in the night, an alluring lover, beckoning, who magically eradicates the choice not to follow. On a quest, one pushes away from overly cultivated beaches, tears away from the fabric of the familiar matrix, and throws oneself into turbulent seas, unknown, unexplored, like the unmade bed of a magic stranger. Fear slowly penetrates a still-intoxicated dawning awareness too late to scramble back across last night's threshold where some all-too-charming image of desire abducted the entrenched life. Loss now means departing from an outer situation, saying one's good-byes, and entering into a fascination that, if successful, brings a completely different perspective into consciousness.

When a provocative interest sweetens the field of one's activity, as with a new course of study or expertise, a fresh idea for an artistic project, or, most prevalently and most powerfully, a new love intrigue, one follows in an enchanted haze of curiosity. Of course loss ensues when the previous structure of one's place in the world must dissolve in deference to the new project.

Consider the case of a comfortable and polite marriage that meets and exceeds the creaturely needs of the couple but offers little opportunity for the kind of healthy tension that breeds passion and romantic encounters. Such a marriage lacks creative vitality: a spiritual relationship that inspires intellectual, emotional, and erotic connections. This situation invites the fortunate encounter with the uncanny, whether in the form of time-absorbing activity or a provocative stranger. When life's core experience leaves the soul asleep in the tower, an eventual awakening gathers. However, feelings of anxiety, isolation, disorientation, and unfamiliarity may accompany this awakening. When the marriage situation dissolves, a previously secure, perhaps even supportive home base also crumbles, leaving only a cloak of discontented expectation for shelter. Here, I mean an irreconcilable marriage, one that has served its time so that both partners may find a more appropriate situation. Many marriages lose their vitality after years of challenge and grief. There is also joy that accompanies many long-term relationships; however, these couples often harbor seeds of renewal dormant within their bond and face the call to renew the relationship that now has a certain ethereal substance. They must then submit to the trials of initiation. In the midst of inner conflict, a distant impulse gradually takes hold, the larger Self waiting to more fully express itself, to blossom.

Containing the Tension

When an intrapsychic conflict begins to capture psychic energy into an area of subliminal tension, an individual will, even without much awareness at first, make subtle adjustments in lifestyle. The situation worsens when the conflict, imaged by mythic battles such as the one Luke Skywalker and Darth Vader fought on the ledge of an abysmal futuristic cavernous interior, draws more and more of the psychic energy available to consciousness deep into the struggle. Here the second phase described by Jung, containing the tension, enters the arena of apprehending the call. The initiate must endure contact with intrapsychic apparitions and experiences long enough to discern their messages and find the threshold through which to attain "resurrection to a new mode of being" (Eliade 1958, 91). Such apprehension often arrives through tremendous dream images or waking visions that tend to overcome the dreamer, demanding attentive humility. Eventually, and perhaps regularly, in every life a conflict arises between "the life we live and the one we have forgotten," which demands attention. Jung insists that our prehistoric past does not impose itself into awareness without sufficient impetus, presenting a dilemma as to whether we have a responsibility to consider the possibilities inherent in that life we have forgotten (Jung 1961, 246).

Murray Stein, in his article "On Modern Initiation into the Spiritual," recounts Jung's experience with the imaginal figures Salome and Elijah, accompanied by a black snake. Jung is curious at first but then becomes skeptical when the young and beautiful Salome, who is blind, insists that Jung is the Christ and can restore her sight. According to Jung's account as reported by McGuire, Jung saw the serpent moving toward him, closer and closer, until it circled around him up to his heart and pressed him in its coils. As he struggled he noticed that he had been forced into the position of crucifixion, sweating streams of water which flowed down all around him. Salome rose and could see. While the serpent pressed, Jung felt that his face assumed that of an animal of prey: a lion or tiger (Jung 1989, 96).

Jung's seminal vision activated a healthy skepticism toward being identified with Christ, revealing his humility, together with an inner command that he attend to the figures and their terrifying autonomy. The vision hints at the profound sacrifice Jung's life subsequently exacted: a life devoted to tracking the unconscious and discerning a healing process. Jung's vision came at a time of deep grieving over his break with friend and colleague Sigmund Freud (Stein 2007, 96). Knowing that his position in professional society would change, he remained devoted to the inquiry extant in a series of visions and active imaginations that mapped his destiny. The sound of the call, of vocation, imaged viscerally through a terrifying ancient drama, fueled Jung into a process endured through determination, curiosity, and faith. When we encounter our own disconcerting images we are never sure whether order will gather within the chaos, whether vague outlines will resolve into image, and certainly we can only hope that clarity will emerge out of the fog. Ryan observes

> that at a very early period of Jung's life, his psyche bodied forth, in the very same grammar of symbols which so often characterized the Shaman's initiatory experiences, a premonitory vision of the archetypal creative substratum of human experience which was to call Jung and act as his daemon throughout his life. (2002, 219)

I am reminded of a dream, one of many in my personal collection, in which daemons and spirits appear as snakes.

The place is remote, undefinable, but something like early American days. There is a large old wooden wagon but no horses. I see an adolescent blonde man pick up a snake behind the neck. It is obviously very poisonous. I feel frightened just watching. Then I turn to someone and ask if they saw how that guy held the snake. Then, as if my observance attracts its attention, the same snake is in a tangled, writhing knot on my right shoulder. It has a pattern of earthy brown colors. I feel powerless, resigned to some insurgent fate—it has all the power to decide whether to bite me or not. Then I see another snake coiled around my left arm at the wrist. It has an exotic translucent green color but also seems deadly.

I have grown accustomed to the ominous appearance of snakes in my dreams and seldom react any longer to their uncanny appearances with terror and aversion. This particular dream seemed unremarkable at the time. Now, however, I understand that the dream, which arrived at a time when the goal of my training felt distant, may have been calling me back to my work, which had acquired its own life and relationship with my myth.

The snake may image the most complete symbol of initiation. Its bite heralds constellation of an unconscious content, that is, a call to apprehend an instinctive potential never before expressed, a power or ability you did not know you had. In the shedding of its skin, we find the transformational crisis, a state of confusion during which all of life gathers and fights, writhing and twisting to free itself and reveal a renewed approach to life or to wither without a struggle. The snake's venom has since time immemorial meant the poison that in a fractionated dose could bring the cure, the potion needed to body forth into a liberated new life, open to the work which calls upon a new idea.

Living the symbol of snake means to me that I must endure, respect, and at times charm the unconscious. Any effort to discern the call requires containing the tension created by inner conflict long enough for the message to reveal itself. Jung explains:

> The struggle between the opposites would persist in this fruitless way if the process of regression, the backward movement of libido, did not set in with the outbreak of the conflict. (Jung 1948a, par. 62)

When the individual meets with a seemingly insoluble conflict and, rather than react by escaping the problem in any number of conditioned responses, struggles within the paradox of the situation, a measure of libido, or life energy, naturally flows into the effort. Suddenly, one finds less vitality for attending to the demands of everyday life. Many initiatory imperatives fail at just this juncture, when the individual feels overwhelmed, then reacts with the same outworn patterns. The old skin remains, like a tattered old cloak, around the smoldering conflict. I once spoke with a woman who was in love with someone who could not fully embrace her. She relegated her therapy sessions and her dream life to a low priority, continuing to wring her hands and respond to the situation with the same old hope that the lover would have a change of heart. Finally, she just quit coming to the therapy sessions. Years later I met her by chance at a coffee shop. The woman spoke to me about the lover in the exact same way, using some of the identical phrasing she had used during our sessions. Nothing had changed. Imagine the effect such a situation could exert on one's physical condition.

The dream cited earlier of execution by skinning (p. xx) exemplifies the snake's influence in my life. A deep conflict between the life I live and the one forgotten has erupted regularly, commanding a shedding of skin almost as autonomous as nature's way with the snake. Each skinning formed, and continues to form, a new fractal that contains the essential story of my life, but each time lived with greater experience, knowledge, and maturity. The bite of the serpent has impelled me to make decisions that rational thinking might consider foolish, even immoral, resulting in considerable suffering. However, the mythic essence of the inner experience interlaced with the narrative of the outer story brings meaning and a sense of purpose to an existence otherwise disappointed in many ways. I find that every person's life unfolds around a central story, a personal myth that more nearly reveals the individual than do the accounts of those memorable events of outer life that find their way into the analytical space. These personal myths, the meaningful stories that seem to determine the course of one's entire life, dwell at the core of initiation; they sing the call, whisper the felt sense of one's soul, and mold the symbol which carries the initiate forward with a renewed sense of meaning and intention for life.

My seemingly meaningless, almost bizarre dream creates a distinct contrast between deadly snakes and the blonde puer, or eternal youth. Just as the beautiful Salome in Jung's dream creates a feeling of uncanniness in such immediate proximity to a huge black snake, the young animus figure in my dream also seems surreal in his relationship to the snakes. One might ask, How did he acquire the ability to charm snakes?

Is he simply a foolish youth, or has he somehow found or developed a deep simpatico with nature? These snakes echo the qualities of creative innocent spirit as well as a connection with earth and the new green of spring. Jung embraced the symbol represented by the snake in its unique ability to join seemingly unrelated aspects of the unconscious: a terrifying and unpredictable instinct juxtaposed with natural spontaneous wisdom that carries archetypal potential to imbue its subject with a penchant for healing (1954c, par. 448). Even though the numinous young man in my dream seems undaunted, the dream ego feels rather anxious, with no choice but to submit. The archetype of initiation proceeds in just the same way. One has no choice but to submit or be destroyed.

A dream which came to me with frightening eschatological implications also exemplifies a message conveyed in dream imagery of a spiritual conflict not yet available to realms of consciousness. At the time of the dream, grief over the dissolution of a relationship that had caught my very soul permeated all conscious experience. The dream presents a scene that contains the insistence of a command.

> *This place seems like a huge cavern, but otherworldly or celestial in nature. I am observing primal forces of good and evil fighting, as if in a science fiction movie. The images are vague but retain an anthropomorphic character; "good" robed in white, "evil" in black. An ominous feeling suddenly grips me that the situation may pose a threat if I stay here. Moving, I find that I can fly, but as soon as I move I realize I was right about the threat. The dark evil force moves in pursuit of me. Immediately the force of light positions itself over my body, protecting me. I look ahead and see that the wall of the cavern has started to peel back like the center of a sheet of paper with a fire burning it from behind. I know if I can make it though the opening I will be free, and moreover, an awareness tells me that I will get through.*

I felt the impersonal, archetypal nature of the dream, wondering what in the earthly realm this dream might be trying to convey. Consumed with grief regarding loss of my lover, I could not imagine attending to a spiritual crisis beyond it, a crisis more essential to my nature than the one at hand.

In her book *On Dreams and Death*, Marie-Louise von Franz offers a description of pictures from the Middle Ages that depict death "as a devil and an angel fighting for the soul of the dying" body, and she further explains that fight scenes, especially duels, appear frequently on

ancient stone coffins. Additionally, she tells us that the gladiatorial battles of old Rome were originally fought in honor of deceased dignitaries
(von Franz 1998, 21–22).

I am alive to report that the dream was not about a person for whom
physical death was imminent. It does, however, suggest a symbolic
death, the immortal soul still the wager. Dreams make no distinction
between symbolic death and physical death. Rather than the end of
an incarnation, the dream figures fight for the soul of an outworn self
whose naïveté would no longer fit into a life demanding an expanded
consciousness and maturity.

When one's heart completely opens to love, the soul bathes herself
in a deep pool of feeling. Prepared by this alchemical ritual of bathing,
she awaits her lover. When the outer relationship cannot continue, the
soul must find love from within or she faces grave danger. One dares not
take a stance of victim, accuser, punisher, or avenger. When one's heart
is broken, the love experienced still lives, independent of the object (the
person loved). If those ecstatic moments that seemed so precious at the
time are to survive with meaning and significance, the one who loved
must gather the love back into a grieving heart and allow the soul to
live. My dream suggests that even though I was not aware of the fighting
forces, a powerful current of life ushered me to safety.

Multiple diversions manifest which assist the reluctant ego to ignore
a call from within and continue in familiar patterns. Overcome with apprehension, an individual facing the challenge of dramatic change may
retreat into addiction, create a tangle of perceived duties, or enter into
some trite new interest. Fear of taking the fateful step has the power
to paralyze revelation of one's essential nature for an entire lifetime.
Countless modern women seethe with masked rage because a seemingly well-founded fear prevented them from leaving the security of a
confining role of caretaker to discover the vitality of their own creative
feminine nature. Similarly, countless modern men suffer in "man caves"
of stagnant depression and constant anxiety because burdening responsibilities keep them from devoting part of themselves to their own creative spirit.

The impetus to cut away dead limbs of reactive habits, shed outdated
garments of a faded persona, and abandon outworn ego attitudes may
require separating from family, leaving a career to which one has devoted valuable resources of time, energy, and money, or confronting time-
honored value systems; it may even require all of these. Inner voices
shout accusations and warnings from age-old thrones of authority while

the call insists upon disidentification with slings and arrows of past disappointments, as well as crowns and silks of past achievement. Following one's daemon, or inner imperative, exacts devotion to an authentic, self-renewing life lived according to the command of an inner authority whispering its summons beyond the cacophony of naysayers, whether from within or from influences in the outer world. The daemon requires one's willingness to continually sacrifice that which no longer invigorates and inspires unique élan. I use the term *command* here in the same sense that Heidegger explains it:

> "to command" basically means, not to give commands and orders, but to commend, entrust, give into safe-keeping, keep safely. To call means: to call into arrival and presence; to address commendingly. (1968, 118)

Admittedly, grief permeates the initiatory way with a well of tears formed from all that one must sacrifice, leave behind, give away. However, when loss invades one's life, in whatever form or amid whatever circumstances, one is challenged to inquire, "What *calls* me into arrival and presence?"

Loved ones are unavoidably affected. If one in a partnership seeks a larger life, the other also necessarily faces the challenge of initiatory crisis. When I left my marriage, my husband took himself into analysis and subsequently met a lovely woman with whom he shared much, and he married her. He grieved at first when our marriage could not go on but met the challenge to self-reflection with an open heart.

Kelly

Kelly, who seeks analysis to explore her fears of confronting an unfulfilling marriage, had a dream wherein she and her husband are about to ritualistically enter a cave along with others. She notices a figure, which is herself, emerge from the cave carrying a candelabra made of twigs. The dream suggests that Kelly cannot enter the cave of initiation without her husband. He will necessarily be affected when she enters into an inner connection that could result in heightened self-confidence together with courage to explore interests heretofore set aside in favor of the duties of wife and mother. The figure coming out of the cave anticipates a potentially promising and creative outcome: a light source fashioned with nature's materials. Kelly felt encouraged by the dream, and what started as a tear-filled session ended with a renewed resolve to stay with the work and gather strength to enter the cave. Through containing conflicts inherent in the prospect of perhaps leaving her marriage and certainly changing her role in the marriage, she engaged with images emerging from the unconscious. Kelly has found courage she thought had escaped her existence altogether.

Beatrice

Derailed by divorce from a confining marriage, Beatrice felt lost in her second marriage. She had met the man who later became her new husband shortly after the divorce but before she had completely reclaimed her strength as an independent, intelligent, and talented woman. Soon after finding her first abode for single life, Beatrice suffered deep conflict about having to live apart from her adolescent son, who depended on her for emotional support, but at the same time she felt drawn to her soul's call to develop her longings for study and teaching and writing. Then one night, anguished over her suffering son to the point of returning to the marriage that had kept her from realizing a responsibility to her own life, she had a dream.

> *I awaken from sleep in the small cottage where I lived when I initially separated from my husband. I feel an overwhelming desire to return to my husband and my son. Walking out, I encounter a very long stairway, seemingly never-ending. I go back inside, then decide to go out again. The stairway again seems to descend unceasingly, but I finally reach the street, whereupon I find that my car is missing. A family of African-American people reassure me that everything is okay and that I should return to my bed. The morning will bring different feelings. I obey them.*

This dream came several years before Beatrice entered analysis, but served as an initial dream for her work. To her surprise, the morning did bring a renewed sense of resolve and well-being. She took the dream as validation and encouragement for her decision to separate from the marriage and as reassurance that the near-terrifying challenges inherent in the transition would be manageable. Beatrice obeyed her own law. The African-American people, embodying (according to her associations) her own untapped vitality dwelling in the unconscious, felt safe to her, offering an attitude of protection, courage, and survival: an unmistakable awareness of the soul's command. She suffered painful accusations issuing from husband, son, family, and, not least, her own inner voices. When her intrapsychic reproach, hushed by repression, finally gained enough power, Beatrice found herself in a terrifying crisis. Even then she came away with a resolve to seek support and guidance through analysis and to confront the ghosts.

Call issues from depths of a forgotten soul, and spirit seeks its expression like an arrow that knows its target, threatening all the unexamined, superficial, outworn, destructive structures that get in its way. Or, conversely, call weaves a provocative tapestry that speaks in the language of destiny, offering a life in the service of a visionary directive that "makes no sound," in exchange for the criticism, the fear, the depression, the anxiety. Pursued by an inner imperative, which springs from the ever-present core of Self, one must turn around, endure encounter, hear the proposal.

Beatrice experienced a confrontation by the unconscious. She found a place in the analytical container where warring forces in her psyche could have a stage and where she could differentiate her own reality from social mores and family prejudices. Heidegger further asserts that "calling offers an abode" (1968, 124). An initiate embarks on the journey to find an abode, a dwelling place for the soul's work, a temple where routine task, through devotion, becomes ritual. The mystery of sacred space enters profane life and brings meaning into everyday experience. Inspiration engenders creative endeavors. This can then gestate where peace pervades the growing "child" and divine love abides. One can wish peace and love for everyone, and may step into it in a myriad of human situations, both joyous and tragic. It may happen in a place of worship or be found momentarily in the way spring leaves tremble in the breeze or at sunset on a gold sand beach radiant under the ball of fire getting nearer and nearer but then peacefully falling into unfathomable depths. These are moments when divine and human seem to intermingle, to melt together. But only the inner temple abides, perpetually and eternally; only construction of the inner temple out of old parts, rededicated to the pursuit of meaning, stands ever and always available.

Al

Al, a man in his sixties, entered analysis after a post-surgery depression brought him to his knees. The surgery, a risky back operation, was remarkably successful, but Al suffered a physical arrest that subsequently developed into a diagnosis of chronic fatigue syndrome. During our first session he explained to me how he finally set out to seek answers rather than relief. For him, relief would take him into his habitual drinking patterns, which he knew to be temporary relief at best, or into a medicated fog of psychopharmaceuticals. He began to read all the esoteric wisdom he could find that might offer some hope. This quest for knowledge led Al to discover books written by Jungian analyst James Hollis about suffering and the psyche. He reported to me that these books changed—even saved—his life. Al contained his conflict by inquiring into the aspects of his illness that medical science could not explain. So, in the face of enormous financial challenges created by prolonged inability to work, Al entered into analysis in an attempt to understand the events of his life, answering the call to a more demanding yet larger life.

Initiation implies just this: death of an existing ego attitude and rebirth of a new attitude made larger by the ego's encounter with, and the soul's relationship to, spiritual allies met in dream and active imagination—what traditional cultures experience as visitation by ancestors. Psychologically, one must endure a confrontation with the unconscious, the "place of ancestors" for modern people. Jung's own life conflicts, together with his seemingly insatiable thirst for knowledge, activated images and encounters in the unconscious that set him on a lifelong search for parallels and meanings. His pioneering courage and tireless investigation into his own experiences as well as those of his patients prompted his conviction that good psychic health may depend on apprehending the unconscious and enduring one's trepidation long enough to follow some of the psyche's extraordinary meanderings even though the meaning continues to confound us (Jung 1944, par. 247).

Those who receive the call through illness often experience regret, feeling a sense of resignation. Opportunity, however, stands every bit as present, every bit as potentially creative. Al has embraced his chronic illness as a chance to listen to nature, his own soul, and to learn to play music on the traditional flutes he has masterfully carved and given as gifts for years. He has set out to walk an inner labyrinth of the same outward life.

Doran

Doran entered analysis seeking relief from troubling grief after the death of her father. Nagging mysteries surrounded his life. Her call to connect with recent ancestors set her on a mission to explore events associated with her father's chronic depression and to redeem, through her own creative process, a relationship with the family homestead that her father had sold under financial duress years earlier. Hers was a detective story which she followed with unmatched will. She diligently followed dreams and synchronicities, carefully recording everything. She searched courthouse records, she walked the land, she created a film and assembled an exhibit of photographs which appeared at the local cultural museum—all of which required several trips to California from Texas. The land is now a Napa vineyard, and the old house is now occupied by a renter. Doran contacted the renter, a solitary man, who was more than happy to allow her to explore the house, where she found records and artifacts belonging to her paternal grandmother and her father. She sat in my office, tears coursing down her cheeks, as she realized that her father had become ill when her mother had insisted, in light of impending financial difficulties, that he sell the land belonging to his family for generations. He had sold his soul. Doran, then in her early sixties, recovered part of her own sense of self through the tremendous effort to understand her father's suffering, thereupon channeling the released energy into schooling at Pacifica Graduate Institute. She continues to harbor an intense yearning to move back to the Napa area. Contacting the ancestors became a personal quest for Doran, serving the goal of transforming her attitude toward herself and toward life.

Doran's call followed the death of her father. In my experience with clients I have found that the death of a parent catapults one into reflections and insights too painful or too obscure to address while the parent survives.

Hal

Hal's mother died a few years after he entered analysis. He had devoted many hours to the process of understanding how early experiences of her continued to influence relationships with women. Not until his mother died and he quickly spent his inheritance was he able to step across the threshold into a more complete sense of his own core identity. For the first time in his life, in his mid-fifties, Hal was able to become responsible for his physical, emotional, and financial well-being. He stopped smoking, started on a regular yoga practice, and began to seriously participate in the Zen group he had obliquely followed for years. He even demonstrated exemplary performance at his job, which had long outworn the interest it held for him. His loss ushered Hal into a richer relationship with his individuality and a greater enthusiasm for all his endeavors.

Call makes an appearance at any age and amid any situation that has grown stagnant. Even the advent of one's mortality constitutes another call. Jung observed that midlife invariably stages a series of scenes, psychic as well as phenomenal, that provoke the insurgence of transforming powers. However, I find that the psyche continually renews itself, sending an individual, at any age, into a litany of deconstruction: a painful skinning that reveals a skeleton ready to grow a new skin.

Outer vocation, as with the call of the shaman, comprises only one of the avenues through which consciousness enlarges through initiation. The psyche seeks to express itself through a number of portals in an attempt to expand existence to its utmost within the limitations of a given individual. To reiterate the various calls into initiatory struggle, other than changing or shouldering the professional robe: (1) one may enter initiation through encounters with eros (in general, a connecting principle), which blossoms through relational awareness; (2) spiritual contents may come into awareness and precipitate an imaginal exploration that ushers one into an expressive arena perhaps never before attempted; (3) inner vocation, that is, devoted calling, blossoms within the solitude of the initiatory vessel; and/or (4) loss of a relative, a pet, or a life situation catapults one into the cave of grief. Herein one encounters a soul space which commands sacrifice of an outwardly focused relationship in deference to an inwardly focused relationship with one's self. Keep in mind that unraveling the four modes of initiatory wandering proves futile in the experience itself; all of them may entangle again so that the initiate suffers in a chaotic cloud of all four situations.

Everyone knows the stories of fateful encounters with eros. No matter the outcome, whether one lives for a time in relationship with the object of desire or not, both parties emerge changed. In the story of Eros and Psyche, when the errant lamp oil awakens Eros and sends him flying, Psyche finds herself faced with daunting tasks. In one version Eros is exiled by his mother, Aphrodite, to stay with the goddess Sophrosyne, who represented a "spirit of moderation, self-control, temperance, restraint, and discretion . . . [a philosophical ideal maintained by the ancient Greeks] perhaps best expressed by the two most famous sayings of the Oracle at Delphi: 'Nothing in excess' and 'Know thyself.'"[3] In modern language one could say that Aphrodite has relegated her son to a treatment center. Psyche could perish into shame and a hardened heart at any stage of the trials, but she perseveres. Eros, having experienced his own challenged exile returns, now more mature, and the *coniunctio* continues on Mount Olympus, transcending ego-absorbed doubts and expectations.

The story of initiation of a spiritual content unfolds in profound dreams or visions or somatic experiences of otherworldly wisdom which eventually find expression in some form of art: writing, painting, sculpture, dance, music, craft, or devotional practice. Keep in mind that the expression may come to fruition many years or even several decades after the actual experience. For example, the female mystic Julian of Norwich started writing almost twenty-five years after her life-altering visions of Christ in the throes of crucifixion, and Gopi Krishna wrote of his debilitating kundalini experience more than twenty years after onset of the trauma. A vision revealing something of one's spiritual core inevitably culminates in an ordeal that brings one's faith in the newly discovered wisdom to the very edge of existence. One meets the challenge with humility and sufferance during which the symbol announces expanded perspective, or one crumbles in disappointment and bitter cynicism.

The story of a calling into the discipline of devotional practice often begins during an intentional introversion wherein one emerges from solitude with the fire of enthusiasm that inaugurates a new way of life. The new way of life, however, blossoms only after an initiatory crisis during which a recapitulation and dispensation of the former life prepares one for the new life. The pitfalls of following an alluring new devotional practice may bring the follower to devastating disappointment. Profound wisdom promises to rewire one's body, mind and spirit. However, if naïve adherence to the precepts brings one to a place of deserted emptiness (as opposed to emptiness alive with potential), discipleship dissolves into petty criticisms, and one wanders aimlessly without a ground.

Not one person escapes the story of grief over loss of someone or something very dear to their heart. The surviving individual has changed profoundly during the life of this loved one or inspired way of life. Their departure means searching one's soul to find the symbol that brings the relationship into its full meaning and impact on one's life. Only through initiatory crisis will a symbol emerge into expression. Grief accompanying loss of a loved one, whether person or life situation, often arrives after the survivor ushers the dying one to the very edge of the threshold of death. Profound confusion ensues, during which one must suffer complete revisiting of life and relationship and meaning. Grace may seem distant, on the other side of an engulfing sphere of perplexity. The situation insists on untiring discernment of one's own essential pillar of significance. However, one may settle in some dark apartment of the sphere where despair prevails and remain unavailable to grace.

Each one of the foregoing initiatory processes may result in failure, that is, one fails to survive the trials inherent in suffering and withers in a lonely darkness of self-pity, bitterness, grief, disappointment, or loss of hope and faith. Perhaps some inability inherent in the situation or in the character of lover or beloved results in disappointment of expectations, felt as a broken heart. The brokenhearted one faces the challenge of suffering agony while remaining open to the symbol that will permeate the whole experience with meaning, but if the agony gains the upper hand, a broken heart becomes a broken life.

When we feel tense, anxious, restless, depressed, vague, or exhausted, we could be at the threshold of transformation, of a call to a larger life teeming with energy, intention, and promise. When life seems flat, uninteresting, completely routine, or too narrow, we are circling the field of call. When loss has us feeling robbed, directionless, purged, or even relieved but misplaced, we might be wandering in the maze of call. When we stumble upon a new idea, a new interest, and different perspective, or even a new lover, we may look around and discover an unplowed field of call.

When we feel that our lives no longer make sense, we no longer feel connected to our daily universe, our value systems no longer contain us, swamps of lassitude prevail, perhaps a crisis is brewing; we then may, amid the turmoil, hear a distant voice call our names. In the words of singer/songwriter/poet Leonard Cohen, "Love calls you by your name." We may dream of setting sail, of embarking on a trek into unknown lands, of hitchhiking in a faraway place, of receiving a secret instruction, of standing at the edge of a cavern ready to descend, of standing at the foot of a mountain ready to climb, or of dwelling in a monastery amid nature, contemplation, and one's own inner tranquility. Hearing the call requires silence; answering it requires courage with a sprinkling of innocence; manifesting it requires walking the razor's edge.

2

Negotiating the Crisis

*The dead and buried become trees who lift up their arms
to call the deaf. With their long fingers and green tongues,
they divulge the secrets of the Earth's heart.*

—RUMI

The immense prerequisite to resurrection, the agony of crucifixion, pales in resurrection's ecstatic glow, but when a call gains momentum the forces of destiny move toward your long and dark night of the soul. A test of faith ensues that brings on a questioning of your trust in people, devotion to systems of thought, or adherence to values that have not undergone scrutiny by your own rational discernment. Understanding and attending to the immensity of these processes remains crucial to realizing their imperative. Answering the call with the devotion of an alchemical adept brings the only reward worthy of life, that is, resurrection, rebirth, renewal. The price is life itself. My dream of execution by skinning without anesthesia (p. xx) suggests the depth of pain lurking in transformation. The motif of execution is no stranger to dream life.

Zoe

Zoe, a lively woman in her fifties, entered into analysis just before marrying a man with whom she had fallen in love. She had spent the first half of her life raising a son as a single mom and exploring a variety of creative interests. Chiefly, she had achieved success as a playwright and looked forward to devoting more time to her talent for writing. Her mother had died not long before she came to see me, and Zoe wanted to make peace with the terrible memories of her mother's emotional illness. After relocating to Scotland with her new husband, who is a Scottish citizen, Zoe brought a dream that held remarkable similarities to one of my own, cited in the introduction, in which I am about to be executed because I have committed a crime against the state.

I have committed a crime of conscience which was hatched on a large
university campus. I drove the getaway car and with the rest of my
"friends" arrived at a majestic place—a rambling old farmhouse in the
south of France. There I waited for the police. At the end of the day I saw
my friends being handcuffed and taken to jail. I got a prison haircut and
changed my clothes before the police came and handcuffed me.

I find a striking resemblance to my own dream in the crime of conscience motif. Also in both dreams the ego goes placidly toward punishment with a passionate, heroic, and stoic resolution. Obviously the crime was a success—the execution meaningful. It was a necessary crime against the establishment or, in my dream, "the state." Initiation recognizes that the established attitude, the state of things, will deteriorate to the point of a vanity that imprisons innocence—like Rapunzel in the tower or Snow White in the dungeon. This identification with superficial evaluations of life must die.

Succumbing to criminal execution in the service of life's continued renewal forms the very core of myth the world over. It articulates numerous images of torture in service of resurrection or knowledge: Christ suffered nailing to the cross in his destiny to redeem a culture that had grown rigid, power-driven, and split between rulers and peasants, initiating a new world order of immense proportions. St. Peter (another crime of conscience, brutally punished) insisted upon crucifixion upside down in deference to the Christ. Odin, the creator god in Norse mythology, hung upside down from the world tree Yggdrasil, whereby he received the mystery of the runes, a primal alphabet that provided a revolutionary form of communication while retaining the mystery in its use as a provocative oracle. Myths involving a hanging sacrifice bring into focus the suspension between opposites that forms the core of our human condition. Anyone who attains a state of equilibrium has sacrificed the conditioned ego-self to a more expanded awareness that allows for a broader attitude toward life, that is, a larger self. One may attain this rare stasis through any discipline that requires contemplation, however, suffering and sacrifice accompany both paths. Sacrificing oneself to oneself necessitates a symbolic death and subsequent rebirth of a conscious attitude fueled by the wisdom attained during the struggle. Osiris was dismembered and his parts scattered (a process later believed by Christians to block resurrection of the body), but the powerful goddess Isis accomplished his resurrection by submitting herself to the humility of searching and gathering. Yet modern individuals separate themselves from the meanings offered by mythical motif, clinging relentlessly to their identity with an ego whose very nature employs the status quo and fears the unknown, positioning itself as the greatest obstacle to growth. Consequently, growth through initiation insists that the very core of consciousness regularly submit to execution, crucifixion, dismemberment, annihilation.

Sacrifice always precludes the journey through darkness and threatens to spoil the effort, either sending the initiate back to the old life, the old suffering, and the old habits, which will certainly feel like death, or forward, most of the time through a symbolic death and renewal (but possibly even into physical death). However, an act of will—that is, conscious sacrifice and determination to endure a crisis that proceeds in the presence of awareness—offers the chance to live a more meaningful life. Jung noticed that when an unconscious content breaks into consciousness and permeates the conscious situation with an unsettling power of certainty, a challenge arises that demands analytical understanding, but most often the individual loses just that power of discernment and falls to one extreme or another, either wholeheartedly accepting or rejecting out of hand the potent new content (Jung 1935, par. 254).

If, however, the initiate resists the impetus to embrace an extreme position, thus taking some time to weigh the elements, a time of intensity immediately ensues. Now one feels caught in a situation that has no easy solution, much like Odysseus sailing between Scylla and Charybdis because it was the only way home but losing six beloved members of his crew. Crisis has already commenced when call enters one's field of awareness, whether one consciously decides to answer the call or fate seems to make the decision. Members of modern society often find themselves thrust into a process of initiation by transitions in outer life which bring to the fore powerful archetypal powers seeking expression. An initiating shaman knows that a test of intense concentration awaits, involving courage, endurance, and skill. Modern persons, however, who have dispensed with myth, traditional ritual, and spiritual mentoring often step into crisis like stepping into a trap expertly disguised by dirt and grass. Psychologically, energy once available for attaining ambitions or satisfying instinctual drives now regresses to the unconscious, activating a story forgotten, unlived, untold, hidden.

The time of crisis activates spiraling, weaving, and overlapping of several components, including: sacrifice, paradoxical passage, a perilous journey, and torture in darkness to the point of death until some act of grace engenders rebirth. Suffering sacrifice and braving paradoxical passage images the third phase in the flow of psychic energy, that of regression. When psychic energy regresses, a relative sensory deprivation ensues, described by Jung as "vague disgust" rather than a describable depression, characterized by discontent, feeling resistant to everything, an ineffable but excruciating emptiness (Jung 1958, par. 169).

Subsequently, the initiate moves into closer proximity with primordial forces of nature and spirit: with ancestors and visions of past and future and with destiny and the unique quest of an individual life clamoring to be lived. Thus, negotiating the perilous journey as well as torture in darkness expropriates the attention of ego consciousness to the unconscious. When an unconscious content gains enough energy to force itself into awareness, the agony of intense conflict pervades an individual situation. This situation must cease in order that the inexorable psychic processes might renew the conscious attitude—renewal which inescapably changes the circumstances of a life.

Extreme allocation of psychic energy to unconscious chambers exposes an outworn ego attitude to torture by the forces that disempower its willful resistance and tear it apart limb for limb. All seems lost at this point until awareness of an essential beingness, a precious secret, brings a change in the demons of torture. The horrible opportunistic demons become angels of mercy who bestow a magical quality to the torn body, which now may emerge with its secret, an inspiring and fertile symbol. Awareness of one's meaningful secret brings the fifth phase in the flow of psychic energy to the fore, emergence of a reconciling symbol.

The English word *crisis* issues from several roots. From the Latin *crisis*, referring to the turning point in a disease, we often employ the expression "crisis point." The shamanic initiate at the point of demise (e.g., dismemberment, disembowelment, boiling or acid bath) experiences a visit by ancestors who craft a new body. The word *crisis* appropriately implies this turning point toward renewal. The Greek *krísis* means separating, discrimination, decision (Barnhart 1995, 173). Jung's ideal reaction to insurgence of unconscious contents cited above would access all three operations: separating, discrimination, and decision making. Crisis then exists as alpha and omega of the entire process of initiatory suffering. Remember that psychologically an intrapsychic conflict initiates the process of regressing psychic energy. This means separating from daily routine and devoting attention to the issue, discriminating among opposing forces, and deciding courses of action based on information not only extant in the outer life situation but also provided by dreams and other imaginative expressions that serve to heal an ailing soul and mentor a larger life. Hexagram twenty-eight of the *I Ching*, *dà guò* (Great Traverses), describes a crisis. Stephen Karcher's translation refers to "the great transition" and further explains, "Life and death are involved in this step. This is a letting go of the past and the emergence of the power to lead your life" (2003, 234). The Chinese ideogram for *crisis* combines two characters: danger and opportunity. While instinct scans the situation for danger, the human spirit scans for opportunity. Of course ego and its preference for status quo tends to lean toward avoiding change in the face of danger. However, the Chinese ideogram implies that confrontation with danger necessarily precludes any possibility of realizing opportunity. The call to live life according to a different law always means danger permeated with opportunity.

Regression of Psychic Energy

A number of ritual events occur that illustrate the psychic event Jung termed "regression of psychic energy." The events may defy delineation; for example, paradoxical passage may exact a sacrifice in addition to the sacrifice inherent in one's very choice to submit to initiation. I find that each commands its own explanation. Processes which clarify and embellish regression of psychic energy include: sacrifice, paradoxical passage, perilous journey, and torture in darkness.

Sacrifice

Sacrifice exacted through answering the call and received by forces unseen continues in perpetual flow throughout the crisis, like blood flowing over the altar in a sacrificial ceremony. Jung described sacrifice poetically as "being wounded by one's own arrow" (1952b, par. 447), a phrase which recalls the words of Nietzsche's *Zarathustra*, "Spirit is the life which itself cuts into life" (1968, 363). Exploring culture in its juxtaposition of sacred and profane, Eliade links sacrifice with the sacred. He explains that through repeating the archetypal sacrifice, that is, a sacrifice in service of attaining an expanded field of awareness, one inaugurates the divine world which interrupts profane time and allows participation in mythical time (Eliade 1954, 36). When mythical time interrupts profane time, meaning it pervades existence, it offers the ego a renewed attitude composed of compassion, purpose, hope, and creative inspiration.

Whether ritual spilling of blood or loss through braving the passage, sacrifice ultimately means one's life and commands devotion to one or more archetypal patterns clamoring to express themselves through dramatic enactments that seem to rock and toss the all too human individual. In "Retrospect," a chapter of *Memories, Dreams, Reflections,* Jung ponders the sacrifice his daemon exacted, artfully illuminated by a passage from Hölderlin:

A creative person has little power over his own life. He is not free. He is captive and driven by his daimon.

> *"Shamefully*
> *A power wrests away the heart from us,*
> *For the Heavenly Ones each demand sacrifice;*
> *But if it should he withheld*
> *Never has that led to good,"*

says Hölderlin.

This lack of freedom has been a great sorrow to me. . . . But the daimon manages things so that one comes through, and blessed inconsistency sees to it that in flagrant contrast to my "disloyalty" I can keep faith in unsuspected measure. (1961, 357)

Jung's image of captivity by his daemon seems to parallel a motif amplified by Eliade in *Images and Symbols* of the "God who Binds." In this discussion Eliade includes, among many others, the Mithraic ceremony of initiation whereby "the neophyte's hands were bound behind his back with a rope." He concludes:

All these rites express a servile attitude, the believer presenting himself as a slave or a prisoner before his master. The "binding" thus takes concrete form as a mark of vassalage. (1991, 104)

Binding the hands images the ultimate submission, rendering one defenseless and unable to physically assert oneself. The captor takes charge. The crisis of initiation brings the acolyte into submission. I do not mean to suggest here that the ego remains in such a reduced state. However, a necessary capitulation during the time of crisis brings the ego into a conscious deference to a sense of purpose for one's being, one's destiny. Successfully accomplishing the initiation ordeal forms an inner relationship between daemon and ego, more appropriately expressed as dialogue than binding. Rather than passive or powerless, the ego serves the necessary role of articulating limitation, necessity, and human responsibility. Integration, that is, an interweaving of unconscious imperative and existing conscious situation, requires awareness by an alert ego consciousness.

My own daemon seems to paint a much more dramatic destiny for me than I will ever realize; however, in dialogue I negotiate a strategy that challenges my limits but does not break them. Roughly ten years ago I had a dream in which I awakened within the dream and realized that I had been sleeping on the back of a giant white serpent embedded in the ground. The dream concludes with me somehow holding this serpent behind the head so that it cannot harm me, and then I realize it harbors no threatening intent. This dream carries enormous implications in the image of the serpent, let alone taking into consideration its color and size. At the time of the dream I knew almost nothing about Eastern mythology and had never seen images of Vishnu (which are numerous at any Indian import shop) dreaming the world on the back of the giant serpent. In this dream the serpent that repeatedly presents itself as an image of my essential being attempts to alert me to a spiritual destiny that altogether escapes my conscious situation. I feel that I can receive its wordless wisdom only through an attitude of humility. My adventurous spirit seems to appease this daunting energy, even though my limitations cause me to fall far short of grounding or expressing its potential.

When a client enters my office for the first time, a call has usually already presented itself by loss: of a partner or other loved one, a job, a residence, health, or even some ineffable vitality for life. I know that the person in front of me suffers not only the loss but also a lack of meaning and has yet to experience the full extent of crisis because an enormous sacrifice of a previous attitude and system of response toward life and Self must ensue.

Andrew

Andrew came to me shortly after entering into a serious relationship, the dynamics of which had unearthed issues of insecurity and fears of deep intimacy which he had swept aside and buried under a persona largely dedicated to pleasing others, which quite successfully ingratiated him to most people. A few months later Andrew found out that he had contracted an incurable disease that meant death if he did not seriously assess his lifestyle, what it meant to him, and how it might kill him.

Andrew's call, which the Fates and synchronicity formed into a new love, made itself more loudly heard through threatening loss of health, which demanded a very sobering confrontation of all the practices and addictions that may worsen the disease. One by one Andrew began answering the demands of his call, making life-altering decisions that meant questioning almost every conditioned response to others and to himself he had developed to approach life's many challenges. He examined relationships to family, friends, colleagues, and himself. His relationship with himself included undifferentiated sexual practices resulting in obsessive-compulsive behavior that undermined his exceptional creative life and annihilated his relationships with nature and simple pleasures.

The night after receiving his diagnosis Andrew had a dream:

> I am in attendance at an opera gala to which I have received instructions
> to wear purple. I am talking with a chorus member who has blonde hair
> and entertains me with her humor. Then a beautiful and voluptuous
> woman with long chestnut hair and dark delicious eyes arrives late. We
> are immediately attracted to one another and find a place in a chapel-
> gazebo to be alone. Beginning to have sex I realize she is a hermaphrodite.
> I feel confused, my arousal dampened. We get dressed and emerge to find
> a setting of townspeople who think I am their priest and that I have been
> engaging in illicit behavior "behind closed doors." I feel appalled by their
> accusations and deny them with an almost vehement assurance. Now the
> two women stand, looking like shy, chaste maiden servants.

Purple, a color representative of the Christian times of Lent and Advent, thereby suggesting sacrifice, transition, and birth of new consciousness, also brings together opposite ends, red and blue, of the color spectrum—a resolution of opposites. However, in the dream, the color is still superficial, a suggestion for the attire of performers. The hermaphrodite also images opposites coming together, but the sex act loses its momentum—integration not yet achieved. The dream closes with a tension of opposites—a dishonest priest and two maidens. Andrew faces the task of resolving the unsatisfying and clandestine nature of his sex life with the honest and sincere person he perceives in himself and wants to present to the world. He must experience a dampening of his sexuality so as to focus on his inner-maiden life until the undifferentiated sexual encounter matures and can be integrated. The color purple will then reflect Andrew's new conscious attitude characterized by reaffirmed integrity.

As Andrew came to the realization that his practices had usurped his life energy and made a vow to abstain from such behavior, his dreams revealed feelings and aspects of himself never before known or embraced. Andrew saw the wanderer in himself, one who feels a sense of belonging wherever the spirit leads him; he embraced the inner goddess who loves him lavishly and felt profound love for a heroic brother who accompanied Andrew on his strange and meaningful wanderings into psychic spaces. Andrew reluctantly realized that answering the call meant his life; it meant "nailing" the self he consciously referred to as "I" and offering it up to a deeper relationship with life and earth and love. One day Andrew arrived in my office elated. He could not wait to tell about a ride on his bicycle one sunshine-drenched afternoon during which he experienced an ecstasy of nature and life and joy. I knew Andrew had succeeded in sacrificing his obsessive-compulsive relationship to momentary pleasure that could never satisfy him in order to live his own truth, which had always been saturated with intelligence, creativity, and love.

Paradoxical Passage

Sacrifice inevitably insists that the initiate negotiate passage through an opening undetectable in any profane or mundane dimension of awareness, described by the phrase "paradoxical passage." Departing from daily life one negotiates this ethereal passage, portrayed in myth by numerous images: gnashing jaws of the serpent, Scylla and Charybdis, Symplegades, clashing cloud gates, cutting reeds, rolling boulders, and colliding icebergs, to name a few (Ryan 2002, 183–84).

Harry Potter's passage from the mundane world to Hogwarts, the school for wizards, provides a playful literary image of negotiating the paradoxical passage. In order to board the train for school he must go to Platform 9¾. Harry searches and searches to no avail. Platform 9¾ does not exist in any rational, linear, objective search. Finally he meets up with the mother of several other students, who explains the task precisely. She tells him that all he has to do is walk headlong at the barrier that separates Platforms 9 and 10 and issues an imperative admonishment that he not stop or entertain fear of crashing. Then she offers motherly advice that he work up a running pace if he feels apprehensive. With a child's determination, courage, and faith, Harry does just as he is told and finds himself successfully standing on Platform 9¾ where the train awaits him. Harry's thoughts as the train pulls away from the station express with candid simplicity the spirit that moves one into vocation: "He didn't know what he was going to—but it had to be better than what he was leaving behind" (Rowling 1997, 93, 98).

Often what we leave behind has long since grown old and outworn. We continue in such situations out of fear of what lies ahead, fear of the consequences, fear that someone might get hurt, fear of doing the wrong thing. One might do well, however, to ask how a state of spiritual stagnation could possibly be the right thing.

The Greek hero Odysseus, fueled by the call toward home, successfully negotiated the narrow straits between a six-headed monster and a powerful whirlpool, equal in their capacity to devour his ship. However, while devoting all available resources to avoiding the whirlpool, six of his trusting and devoted crew fell prey to the monster. Successfully negotiating the threatening opposites requires shrewd and vigilant effort to find a weakness through which one can slip undetected. Six members of Odysseus's beloved crew perished. Yet, without braving the passage the voyage would halt, and all accomplishment, all tenacity, bravery, and crafty scheming would go for naught. Not only does the passage take what it will, the sacrifice demanded by such a passage continues, bringing focus and awareness to the renewed existence. Eliade explains:

> this crossing is difficult; . . . not all souls succeed in traversing it; . . . only the "good," and especially the initiates, cross the bridge easily . . . certain privileged persons nevertheless succeed in passing over it during their lifetime, be it in ecstasy, like the shamans, or "by force," like certain heroes, or, finally, "paradoxically," through "wisdom" or initiation. (1964, 483)

Also,

> he who succeeds in accomplishing [the paradoxical passage] has transcended the human condition; he is a shaman, a hero, or a "spirit," and indeed this "paradoxical" passage can be accomplished only by one who is spirit. (ibid., 486)

"Good" in this passage parallels the Hopi belief, discussed in chapter

1, that snakes carry an instinct for the pure of heart. Snakes in this case represent the human capacity for wisdom, intuition, instinctual discernment, and purity of motive. Like the alchemical adept, an initiate successful in safely entering the realm of wisdom possesses certain virtues. In his pioneering work to interpret alchemical teachings, Jung discovered that the wisdom of the alchemists was rooted in fourteen principal virtues: health, humility, holiness, chastity, virtue, victory, faith, hope, charity, goodness, patience, temperance, spiritual discipline or understanding, and obedience (Jung 1944, par. 382).

I can think of a few virtues to add to the list. I find that my own experience demands determination to endure and sustained enthusiasm along with humility, patience, and temperance. Innocent curiosity toward discovery also helps allay fear and fuels forward motion even when emotional and physical resources begin to wane. I encountered Jung's writings while trying to fashion a way to understand my own spirituality. I felt like I had stumbled upon the fountain of *aqua permanens* (permanent water, or holy water) to quench my thirst at the source. An effervescent passion permeated my existence so that all challenge, all obstacles, all fear bowed to some unseen force, clearing the way for further study in Zürich, Switzerland. It all happened, in retrospect, somewhat seamlessly. Each challenge commanded focus and courage, and I always felt surprised when I successfully negotiated any task. I *followed* the call, not knowing or even considering the possible costs, except the obvious financial ones which, even though quite extensive, turned out to be the most insignificant. Suspending rationality, and perhaps also practicality and morality, took me through the paradoxical passage. My outer life intentions and strivings began to serve my thirsty soul and the "I" formerly known became passé.

Psychologically, according to Jung, the individuation process, a series of initiations, requires balance of threatening opposites imaged appropriately by Scylla and Charybdis. A relationship with the unconscious ideally creates an energy which permeates one's relationship to the world, infusing it with vitality, challenging the acolyte to live the reality of life—and its unavoidable suffering—with an enthusiasm that imbues the suffering with joy. Avoiding the pitfalls of valuing either entity, conscious thought or unconscious presentiment, at the expense of the other poses a dire threat. One faces the temptation of losing touch with body and ground and spiraling into the "smoky life" of unearthed spirit or of becoming an evangelical preacher of sorts who reduces the "good news" to uncontemplated justification. I remember a question offered by my analyst in response to a dream image I ruthlessly described as myopic and fundamentalist. She wanted to know how fundamental thought might show up in my life. I abjectly replied that some might categorize me as a fundamentalist Jungian. At the time of the dream I had been in analysis only a few months. I kept a "disciple of Jung" attitude until I found myself caught in a romantic relationship that my dream life swept up into a spiritual awakening of the soul while the outer relationship remained one-sided, largely unsubstantiated. The lover in my dreams resembled the actual man only superficially. My own spiritual essence embodied the dream image, leaving me confused and inexorably drawn to a fallible human who simply enjoyed witnessing my passion. When he'd had his fill and moved on, I landed on the ground as though falling from the moon—shattered. Dismemberment seems like a weak approximation of the fragmentation I felt. I stepped into a spiritual crisis wherein I questioned the value of dreams, of dream work, of life itself. No longer could I or anyone else consider me a fundamentalist Jungian, and, unfortunately, I also found myself with a faltering identity. The motif of having my bag stolen or misplaced littered my dreams. Everything hung in suspension. Only a remnant of faith remained—faith that a seed or essence of truth dwelled among the fragments. At this time I stumbled upon Heidegger's book of the same name, *The Essence of Truth*. I had read volume sixteen of Jung's *Collected Works* years before, but only through suffering the loss exacted by Scylla and Charybdis did I grasp the dangers Jung describes:

> The first is the danger of the patient's using the opportunities for spiritual development arising out of the analysis of the unconscious as a pretext for evading the deeper human responsibilities, and for affecting a certain "spirituality" which cannot stand up to moral criticism; the second is the danger that atavistic tendencies may gain the ascendency and drag the relationship down to a primitive level. Between this Scylla and that Charybdis, there is a narrow passage, and both medieval Christian mysticism and alchemy have contributed much to its discovery. (1946, par. 448)

Similarly, Murray Stein describes what he terms the "twofold movement of individuation":

> the opus of individuation, . . . a psychological imperative, requires reductive analysis on two fronts: on the persona side, it amounts to differentiating oneself from the psychosocial persona and to dissolving the

identity that has built up over time in one's personal history; and on the syzygy side it requires differentiating oneself from the archetypal images and fantasies that emerge and invite grandiose identification as a compensation for what has been lost through the analysis of the persona. (2006, 18)

For my part, the warnings stood clear enough, and of course I intended to avoid at all cost the dreaded "grandiose identification" with archetypal images. However, when Eros beckoned I followed like a bee to heather in full bloom. The inexorable god was in complete control. Describing the various aspects of the Greek Eros in his book *Alchemy of the Soul*, Martin Lowenthal explains, "Great Night also named him Ericepaius ('feeder on heather'), a buzzing celestial bee, carrier and dispenser of the nectar of divinity" (2004, 4). Like the most famous album recorded by the late Jimi Hendrix, my soul repeatedly insists, "Are You Experienced?" Tortured and beckoned by the archetypal forces of rebel, fool, and eros, warnings and taboos never prevented me from following curiosity or passion. Once torn from idealization, the challenge to critically understand and integrate the wisdom of their inflicted suffering apprehends anyone tenacious enough to continue the opus.

Shamans in initiation have learned the taboos of the tribe through elder sponsors or mentors who warn against the mesmerizing powers of the other world, which can be quite threatening to curious naïveté. These mentors (or fathers) hold the initiate in prayerful protection in an effort to discourage harmful spirits. I am thoroughly convinced that my own spiritual survival rested in the wisdom and strength of my analyst. With patience and tenacity he held my shattered soul, unwilling to allow me to entertain even the possibility of collapse. With his discerning and compassionate attitude, he endeavored to keep me in Tao, constantly enticing my focus back to understanding the confusion of events rather than getting carried away in them.

This presents a question that faces our profession. Is the role of the analyst absolutely necessary, that is, can an individual attend a workshop, learn a few techniques grounded in active imagination or dream interpretation, and save themselves a fortune in analysis? I actually witnessed a workshop leader, a published author, Jungian psychotherapist, and professor who interprets mythological motifs, suggest this very solution to the participants, and this person was not the first. In a society that tends to shame and ridicule those who seek therapy and analysis, individuals view the one-on-one dialogue with a therapist as an indication of weakness. They take the attitude that an intelligent, successful, and creative person such as themselves should be able to accomplish this "individuation thing" on their own. Some self-satisfaction may occur at the outset that validates this person's decision. However, the suffering will return, often more intense than ever, and the cycle repeats: another seemingly more sophisticated self-help workshop, another esoteric class, another lofty seminar. Even the most intelligent and creative people, however, will fail to accomplish the intense self-reflection and pruning of habitual responses and subliminal prejudices required to discern conditioned values and behaviors from those of the core self. Among my own clients, I notice that the most gifted and devoted ones, in active imagination, writing, pictures, and dreaming, tend also to devote more resources, both of time and money, to their analysis. They make the most appointments, regardless of financial limitations, and they bring their work, their struggles, and often their tears. I do not think even one of them would deny the value, let alone the necessity, of bringing their conflicts, feelings, and images into the analytical container.

Like the sacrifice, paradoxical passage remains extant in the initiate's challenge. One never gets altogether beyond the temptation to retreat into one opposite or the other, taking up the superhuman identity of an all too willing archetype in an effort to appease a belittled, struggling persona. Symbolically accomplishing the passage during initiation readies the shaman to repeat the journey many times in the course of healing rituals. Getting safely through the paradoxical passage means that all strongly held opinions and polarized viewpoints must enter the ambiguity of question. Values held by society and culture and taken for granted by the individual come under scrutiny. The heavy baggage of culturally formed attitudes must be thrown overboard. Every client who enters analysis initially struggles mightily to examine the many habits, values, and roles that seem second nature; every client faces a challenge to dispense with those that no longer serve life and growth, then reenlist the others. Resistance, the most powerful ego defense mechanism, prevents forward motion. The initiate, or analysand, may feel claustrophobic or remorseful over having entered such a torturous endeavor, thereby sabotaging their healing process and even discontinuing the analytical struggle. A thorough anamnesis of one's life and willingness to question every precept accompanies the arduous crawl to the cave, a place of further torture and reduction where the crux of crisis releases a symbol to inform one's new life.

In the quote cited above, Jung speaks of the "spirituality which cannot stand up to moral criticism." Our Western culture has integrated many teachings from the East: varieties of yoga, various meditation practices, chanting, breath work, healing techniques, and so on, all of which enrich our lives and introduce documented positive results. However, when these practices replace self-reflection and responsibility for one's life, they have been misused and misrepresented. I think this constitutes an example of what Jung means when he speaks of moral criticism. Psychic morality demands the suffering inherent in examining one's life to find the path between identification with and entrapment within outworn orientations and limited perspectives often informed by trauma and wounding. This includes on one hand flying up out of them, rootless, into spiritual preoccupations, or on the other hand (and probably worse) guru projections.

Consider a woman who experienced molestation by a father who was a minister in a fundamentalist Protestant church. He regularly accused her of having a sinful nature and she thus bore an identity permeated with shame and guilt. As an adult she disowned Christianity and its church and joined with followers of a charismatic yogi. Her choice seems predictable and understandable. However, she has sidestepped the suffering of a systematic healing process that could help her to know and love the inspirited, strong, talented woman resting at the core of herself. She has not accomplished paradoxical passage. Such a challenge would mean slipping between the glamour of a false persona, identified as disciple of a relatively unknown man who nevertheless inspires her life energy, and the terrifying threats of a repressed shadow. In the style of a conscious initiation rite, she may then embark upon the perilous journey to the cave where her essential self may make itself known if she has the strength to endure the torture of facing the demonic inner voices which have carried on the deprecations of her father. Through consciously enduring their accusations, which bite at her flesh and tear her apart, she allows and experiences their transformation into helping spirits.

In general, paradoxical passage means slipping between the opposites of the fears that gather around decisions to abandon outworn ways of being in one's body and in the world and the impulse that lures one to the seductive promise of spring and renewed interest in life. Fear and impulse struggle perpetually, creating a veil that prevents the ego from being able even to see the door, let alone use it.

Perilous Journey

Stepping out of one's former life, then, becomes a step through paradox. Rational thought fails, and one enters the path of a perilous journey, often symbolized by a narrow and tortuous passage underground. This may reduce the initiate shaman to a crawl. In concert with passing beyond its gnashing jaws, the initiate metaphorically enters the body of the serpent—the perilous journey—often appropriately comprised of a long and painful crawl. Chauvet Cave in France, which has received remarkable media attention, shows signs of initiatory ritual with a marked dichotomy between an area nearer the entrance and the deepest part, which is separated by a narrow passage (Bahn 2003, 202). This is only a more recent example of a discovery that unmistakably supports the idea that initiates in traditional societies accomplished a tedious voyage to a sacred place where sensory deprivation serves as spawning ground for imaginal stories of torture and healing. Psychologically speaking, the ego's viewpoint submits and dissolves in deference to the meaning of the struggle. Ryan describes another initiation site to illustrate the process of perilous journey, the Mayan Pyramid of the Sun:

> The cave running beneath the pyramid has many arresting features, some of which originally did not belong to the cave structure. The natural course of the cave was purposely changed to make it wind, a path more tortuous (and, perhaps more ritually torturous) and serpentine. In addition, in many areas the cave's dimensions were intentionally constricted and the ceiling was artificially lowered to make the initiates bow, crawl and squeeze their way through. (2002, 213)

Eliade explains:

> The road is arduous, fraught with perils, because it is, in fact, a rite of passage from the profane to the sacred, from the ephemeral and illusory to reality and eternity, from death to life, from man to the divinity. Attaining the center is equivalent to a consecration, an initiation; yesterday's profane and illusory existence gives place to a new, to a life that is real, enduring, and effective. (1954, 18)

In hexagram sixty-two of the *I Ching*, *xiǎo guò* (Small Traverses), Karcher issues a gentle warning: "It is a time for great care with an expectation of great results, the penultimate step. Remember, in this time you are the bird, not the hunter" (2003, 423). Just as a hunted bird must fly low and remain attuned to every movement below, during this phase the initiate keeps a low profile together with heightened awareness, paying strict attention to only the immediate issues, daring not to look back and being unwise to look too far ahead.

Doran

In the course of her analysis, Doran had a dream which suggests a treacherous passage at a time when she had made a decision to study for a master's degree. Just as anticipated by the dream, the challenges inherent in her experiences at the university proved to require every ounce of courage she could muster.

> *I am driving a car along an ocean. The road is very bumpy, in terrible condition—some of it washed away, narrow in places—very treacherous. To the right are dense overhanging sandy walls—cliff-like—and the road is at the bottom of this overhanging cliff. The ocean is really moving— high waves, lots of motion.*

The dream's image, as daunting as it seems, symbolically anticipated without much exaggeration the path she later found herself negotiating. In addition to the demands of study and distance learning, Doran encountered complexities—her own and those of others—that formed a tangle of relationships exacerbating the profusion of academic work. She found that the very tense task of discerning which patterns belonged to her and which belonged with others in her cohort (study group) demanded a formidable measure of psychic energy, emotion, cognitive time, and consideration.

An inner necessity to negotiate paradox and allow its ambiguities both in ourselves and in others seems to position one on a trip along a winding, narrow mountain pass. This is shown in Doran's dream or by anyone surrounded by unrecognizable regions, like Jonah swallowed by the whale. My dream of trying to find the brakes in an old pickup truck lumbering steadily downhill (p. xiii) adds yet another image to the motif of descent. I find that dreams of an uncontrollable vehicle are not uncommon, yet the appearance of the wise man in the passenger seat drew my attention. This dream carried a depth of meaning beyond the typical "my outer life is out of control" association. I felt a touch of the numinous as soon as I turned my perception to this man who meant protection, companionship, witness, and encouragement, as well as insistence on a mission that I had no choice but to accept. Now the descent embodied meaningful intention. Still, one cannot escape the implication of abduction implied. The numinous man had robbed the dream ego of volition, a situation soon to manifest in the intensity of falling in love. Mary Aswell Doll, in an article for the journal *Spring*, offers an insightful psychological explanation of the metaphor of rape or abduction. She explains that when the other world impinges upon an ego too attached to its naïve attitude, a necessary—even fortunate—rape carries the uninitiated identity down to the dark side. There, masters of initiation torture and then reestablish the identity in a more mature relationship to life (Doll 2008, 129).

One endeavors to tolerate and even enlist the opposites, to "integrate unconscious depths with life's surface" (Ryan 2002, 160), not unlike a trek along the razor's edge. The motif of descent describes a feeling of existing in strange surroundings beneath or outside of the normal mechanisms of life. Tensions arise between outer strivings which are often reduced to essentials like eating, sleeping, and grooming, inner wandering, and searching for the unique meaning relevant to the situation at hand. In any case, the descent promises to annihilate all connection to previous persona, identity, and ego attitude so that meaning may permeate existence. Jung finds the purpose of descent revealed in the myth of the hero where the abode of danger (watery underworld, cave, woods, mountain, island, castle, etc.) conceals the "treasure hard to attain": jewel or gold, virgin princess, life potion, victory over death (Jung 1944, par. 438).

Torture in Darkness

It is very probable that the archetypes, as instincts, possess a specific energy which cannot be taken away from them in the long run. The energy peculiar to the archetype is normally not sufficient to raise it into consciousness. For this it needs a definite quantum of energy flowing into the unconscious from consciousness, whether because consciousness is not using this energy or because the archetype attracts it to itself. The archetype can be deprived of its supplementary charge, but not of its specific energy. (Jung 1954a, par. 425n)

Continuing to endure sacrifice, paradox, and the perilous journey brings one into a den of the cave, the womb, a gestation period, but also a time of torture, dissolution, and/or dismemberment. The old and untenable self suffers complete annihilation until the turning point, the crux of crisis when the initiate through grace experiences re-member-ment, rebirth, and resurrection and receives an adamantine or hallowed body. The way leads into a room far below, an interior world where the unconscious re-creates the story of torture, death, and dismemberment. Whether one arrives at such chaos through loss, desire, or both, whether through conscious choice or an unconscious insistence on renewal, one enters a state of confinement, inner torture, even immanent death. Im-ages analogous to scraping away flesh until the body is reduced to skel-eton ensue, and only essence remains. My dream descent to a basement room in an ancient village represents essence in the image of a primi-tive doll, a homunculus figure, a psychological fractal. Such an image is analogous to the kachina doll of the Native American Pueblo tribes, signifying a spirit being, an immanent Self also contained in the Hindu idea of Purusha.

During my own inner torture I unintentionally lost thirty pounds. At 5 feet 7 inches and 110 pounds, I embodied the motif of reduction to a skeleton and found meaning in the uncanny sequence of events that led to such a dramatic manifestation of archetypal imperative. My closet lit-erally represented an old self, which I necessarily released to thrift shops and friends. The skeletal experience left me with only a diffuse aware-ness of the reality of myself. It was an essence which, when imaged by the basement doll, contains only the gamble of life amounting to fate unless relationship to the ancestor who stood in witness prevails. Ac-cording to Eliade,

> One of the specific characteristics of shamanic initiations, aside from the candidate's dismemberment, is his reduction to the state of a skeleton. We find this motif not only in the accounts of the crises and sicknesses of those who have been chosen by the spirits to become shamans but also in the experiences of those who have acquired their shamanic pow-ers through their own efforts, after a long and arduous quest. (1958, 92)

Recall my dream of execution by skinning (p. xx), an unquestionable metaphor for a serpent shedding its skin, as well as reduction to skel-eton. I had committed some "crime" against the state, a state of things that needed an insurgence of love. For fifty years I had lived very little in concert with my true self. For most of my life I had responded to cultural and societal expectations, demands, woundings, and addictive patterns.

Such an abundance of error requires extremely invasive measures. In the dream I had an awareness that at the time of the crime I realized the danger of being discovered, caught, and punished. Decision to commit the crime amounted to a sacrifice of myself, a conscious act in service to something I believed to be of greater importance. I struggled to endure the pain of separation inherent in my psyche's attempt to remember an essential truth or primal endeavor, coupled with a new vehicle of experience. Drawn into the drama of torture, I was faced with surrendering to an autonomous and individual foundation of meaning capable of fashioning an adamantine body and soul; this meant a new relationship to life and death, to achievement and acquisition, to desire and necessity. I finally realized that this shift of attention in negotiating the slings and arrows of mundane life renders one less vulnerable to them.

Sacrifice continues in the darkness of torture. One relinquishes ego identity and lives for a time in a state that seems like dissolution, formlessness: the alchemical *nigredo*. Life becomes myth as one enters the belly of the beast, often depicted in dream and vision, as well as in ritual, by a descent into an area below ground and cave-like. Jung explains:

> We meet dragons, helpful animals, and demons; also the Wise Old Man, the animal-man, the wishing tree, the hidden treasure, the well, the cave, the walled garden, the transformative processes and substances of alchemy, and so forth—all things which in no way touch the banalities of everyday. The reason for this is that they have to do with the realization of a part of the personality which has not yet come into existence but is still in the process of becoming. (Jung 1948b, par. 558)

A sense of *tremendum* permeates existence with its pendulum of numinosity oscillating between terror and ecstasy. A student once asked me, "What do you mean when you say life becomes myth?" I tried to explain that one enters the realm of story where the dream world interweaves with the outer world; where ego notices coincidences that do not seem so coincidental. It is a field of synchronicity and serendipity where meaning overrides logic and where image inevitably takes on the nature of an object of reconciliation, that is, symbol.

When one's former relationship to outer reality vanishes, the former life is lost. Again, in the words of Eliade, the initiate must "break with the universe of daily life" (1958, 101). Psychologically, a person will experience a regression of the psychic energy too long poured into connections to institutions and individuals that have in many ways graced life as well as wounded it. One feels such connections falling away and may grasp desperately to save them, but to no avail. These institutions have provided space for expression of roles and talents which no longer serve the meaning that has gained foremost importance. Former patterns of managing life's situations have little effect in the life of a redefined self. Retrieving oneself from a forest of obsolete roles and passive activities results in an excess of energy strong enough to activate unconscious images. Rather than succumbing to the ensuing feeling of heaviness or lethargy or depression experienced when one's conscious awareness is robbed of psychic fuel, Jung explains that one may gain possession of the misappropriated energy by embracing the emotional situation, settling into it, then expressing in a journal all the images and associations that arise. This discipline begins to compose the cure, bringing information from the unconscious into awareness (Jung 1958, par. 167).

Jung developed a discipline he called active imagination: bringing a focused awareness into dialogue with figures appearing in a setting existing apart from conscious recognition. He then recorded the dialogues and impressions diligently through word and art. Many individuals find the process quite challenging, others simply focus attention inward and immediately notice an ongoing plot that seems to carry on perpetually whether attended or not. As a person learns to devote complete concentration to a play in which the ego is often both actor and audience, the plot reveals itself. However, without successfully stealing into the theater, having no reservation or ticket to present, the play never begins to inform one's life. Here the individual faces a necessary sacrifice of a piece of the conscious position. All previously held beliefs, values, ideologies, teachings, creeds, and dogma hang in suspension, allowing one's awareness to shift toward the creative imagination. Murray Stein explains that active imagination facilitates the analytical movement, a movement which involves a loosening throughout or a breaking up. This slackening process, inherent in individuation as well as initiation, provides a wider space between ego consciousness and persona on the one side and anima/animus, the gendered archetypes of creativity, on the other.

> Through [analytic movement], consciousness and identity come to resemble less a static set of objects and patterns, like a painting, and become more something like a mirror through which objects can float freely into and out of view but do not remain permanently in residence. This movement of analysis includes dissolving the attachments to religious objects, traditional practices, and projected theologies. (Stein 2006, 35)

A feeling of depression, lethargy or drowsiness, sadness or melancholy may pull consciousness into the inner life of imagination. In Doran's case, a flood of emotion emerged—never before fully experienced. In the case of Al, cited in the chapter 1, his surgery brought him defenseless into the depths of depression rooted in childhood when his beloved mother died an untimely death, leaving an eleven-year-old Al confused and heartbroken. Analysis enabled him to connect with Native American ancestry, which then provided inspiration, self-worth, and meaning to his suffering.

Activation of Unconscious Images

> Where everything, world and self, is shadow-like, there is no relationship to the genuinely true and unhidden.... There, man is lacking something. He is sick, and healing is necessary. But healing presupposes the correct diagnosis of the illness. (Heidegger 2002, 27)

If one accompanies the psyche "on some of its strange symbolic wanderings," the tension often relaxes because creative images and ideas fill inner space as conscious attention turns inward (Jung 1944, par. 247). Sadness felt in response to the situations of daily life settles like dust, and the intentional wanderer finds solace within dramas of the inspirited soul. I am reminded of a story told to me by a Native American man who is now a successful mask artist.

Aarnaquq (his tribal name) was a very successful investment banker living in New York. In his mid to late thirties he developed dangerously high blood pressure in response to a fifteen hour per day (or more) work schedule together with a failing marriage. His doctor warned him on several occasions, and finally one day the frustrated doctor took Aarnaquq firmly by the shoulders and told him that he must leave his job or his marriage or both—or he would die. Feeling both too young to die and too young to retire, Aarnaquq finally relented and opted for early retirement. His entire identity was dissolved. During an intense depression he decided to seek healing from his father and grandfather, who were healers in the community of his childhood. They used masks in their healing rituals. Aarnaquq became interested in the masks and commenced an enthusiastic inquiry that took him all over the Americas as well as deeply into the ceremonial masks of his own heritage. Employing styles, techniques, and ceremonial images from various traditions, he designed and created works of art, enlisting the juxtaposition of his ancestral knowledge and his inner experience. Public response to his work led him to art shows and galleries, and at the time I met him at the Fall Market in Santa Fe, Aarnaquq was selling his masks for tens of thousands of dollars.

Aarnaquq's story provides a provocative example of a successful initiation. His call arrived as a warning from the doctor. Crisis followed with the loss of a very successful professional identity and ensuing depression, leading to a journey back to his ancestral roots mirrored by the inner journey to discover an undeveloped part of himself. The synchronistic expeditions culminated in recognition of the powerful symbolic significance inherent in the masks of his ancestors, which gave meaning to his suffering and brandished a transformation when he connected with his soul through reaching out creatively to the traditions of his community and his heritage.

A Samoyed shaman from Siberia cited by Ryan revealed a dream of being dismembered and boiled in a pot for three years (2002, 95). In the throes of dismemberment, a cry for mercy issued from the tortured to the very one(s) who drives the nails, wields the whip, severs the limbs; they are the archetypal force that calls life energy to itself. At the very culmination of crisis, the final demise of the old self, love prevails and provides the fuel for endurance and the courage for redemption. In an unpublished note quoted by Heidegger, Nietzsche states, "love alone will make it right—(the creative love that 'forgets' itself in its works)" (1984, 226). In his "Late Thoughts," published in *Memories, Dreams, Reflections*, Jung explains the importance of love:

> Love "bears all things" and "endures all things" (1 Cor. 13:7). These words say all there is to be said; nothing can be added to them. For we are in the deepest sense the victims and the instruments of cosmogonic "love." . . . [Man] may assent to it, or rebel against it; but he is always caught up by it and enclosed within it. He is dependent upon it and is sustained by it. Love is his light and his darkness, whose end he cannot see. (1961, 354)

Aarnaquq discovered the deep love dwelling within himself that instilled him with an appreciation for ancestral masks, making the situation right by giving him an avenue for exploring a different kind of work—a kind that creates rather than destroys. The love he found and expressed then naturalized to include other relationships in his life.

Only a person suffering an agonizing spiritual insurgence from within would knowingly embark upon the torturous journey of initiation. The imagery described by initiating shamans shocks the reader with horror; however, the silent desperation lived by countless individuals in our postmodern society reveals endless lifetimes of suffering. The real difference lies in the dimension of meaning. An initiate understands the trials of ritual initiation as a sacrifice in service of a meaningful life. Successfully accomplishing initiatory trials connects the courageous one to both a life lived in answer to vocation and a future permeated with destiny rather than blind fate.

In my dream of the ancient doll harboring a pair of dice (p. xiii), the ancestral gentleman bore witness with such presence that I felt profound love. A poem by Anne Sexton lends for me an extraordinary dimension of meaning for the curious dice. In "The Awful Rowing Toward God," she is playing poker with God. She had not heard the announcement of a wild card when He (her pronoun) dealt the cards because she had been awestruck, thus she did not initially realize there was no losing hand. When He calls her wager and they show their hands, she proudly holds a royal straight flush and He fans out five aces. He laughs a laugh that transmits laughter into her, "a Rejoice-Chorus" at their victories. The poet continues with a love note, "Dearest Dealer," and expresses her love for His love, an "untamable, eternal, gut-driven *ha-ha* and lucky love."

I knew in my dream that the divine figure standing there with such an air of nonchalance while I was trembling with anticipation certainly possessed the luck of the dice, and like Anne Sexton, I loved him for it. I knew that, in the end, only his intervention could save the life that I must wager time and again.

In Doran's case, introduced earlier (p. 24), a mystery imbedded in outer events was revealed through her diligent devotion and detailed effort to discover the secrets of her father's property in the Napa Valley. Psychologically, consciousness suspends its power and possessions, its trophies, and even its wounds in an attempt to hear the message of unconscious wisdom (Jung 1952b, par. 671). Submitting to the interests of her unconscious brought Doran through unresolved grief over the death of her father and unlocked a wealth of psychic energy which she channeled into various endeavors, including art projects and educational pursuits.

Emergence of Symbol

We could multiply examples of cases where, at the critical moment, a "saving" thought, a vision, an "inner voice," came with an irresistible power of conviction and gave life a new direction. (Jung 1935, par. 254)

Ryan, in explaining Jung's approach to the psychological component of spiritual calling, explains that a "deeply needed mode of self-expression," for which one often has limited conscious associations, emerges in the form of a "new creative content" (2002, 65).

Lee

Lee, a very insightful, resourceful, and successful woman, remembered a series of very early childhood dreams and imaginings. In the dreams she is the daughter of a family of seals. As a young seal she swims in circular patterns with her seal mother and siblings. She recalls that even at this preverbal time in her life she had an awareness that the seal family represented some reality more important than the human family in which she found herself. These dreams came to her memory after two years of analysis. At that time Lee stood at the threshold of midlife, struggling to understand her life and especially to comprehend an intimate relationship with a partner who often behaved unpredictably and explosively, not at all like her inner symbol of harmony. Remembering these dreams and visions offered valuable insight into impulses underlying Lee's numerous outer life expeditions, which seemed like endeavors to create a family circle. In a relationship that challenged her patience and drained her heart, she struggled to achieve balance and serenity. The archetype of initiation required that she abandon old patterns of trying to attain an outer life expectation of harmony and balance by repeatedly assuming responsibilities within harmful relationships that exhaust creative energies. Her endeavors to manifest the circle in outer life have taken on a self-sustaining rather than self-depleting character now that she has consciously found a way to relate with the perfect family she carries within. Her unconscious drive to bring a sense of completeness to conscious situations connects her with the very stabilizing symbol that brings a truth about herself into existence, as well as a sense of self-assurance to her ego identity.

"The life . . . we have forgotten" emerges in dreams and visions as symbolic story that has an essential aspect often mirrored in myth or fairy tale (Jung 1989, 246). Jung noticed that "restlessness begets mean-inglessness," further surmising that lack or absence of meaning consti-tutes an overarching "soul-sickness" with alarming consequences that our current Western culture has yet to grasp (1934b, par. 815).

> In the same way that the body needs food, and not just any kind of food but only that which suits it, the psyche needs to know the meaning of its existence—not just any meaning, but the meaning of those images and ideas which reflect its nature and which originate in the unconscious. (Jung 1954c, par. 476)

Jung's emphasis on meaning as the primary agent of healing compels one to devote psychic as well as material resources necessary to find the meaning, to redeem, or breathe life into a story that lies outside or before consciousness. Lee intermittently suffered anxiety which fueled insomnia—a "restlessness." She now understands that the suddenly re-membered image of the seal family provides rest for her soul and an open door for her mind to visit. She recognizes her outer entangle-ments as unattainable approximations of the family circle. Now Lee has retrieved some of the energy she expended trying to create an inner image of harmony among fallible humans. Living out of one's harmoni-ous inner image of self brings harmony into an often chaotic world, but the world will always only approximate the vision. Lee realized the im-portance of manifesting her inner image in the world while suspending expectation of perfect harmony.

Kelly

Recall the candelabra fashioned from intertwining twigs in Kelly's dream mentioned earlier (p. 21). This symbol implies fire, a symbol of force, which the ego may experience as a catalyst in creative transforma-tion: as in the act of cooking, illuminating a space, or warming a chill. Conversely, fire may suggest destructive failures expressed by episodes of rage, dry summer fires out of control, or unbridled passion lost in a frenzy. Kelly's dream suggests a creative potential since the fire appears contained in a very innovative candelabra. Kelly in fact does possess an artistic talent, which she routinely expresses through various media. The dream suggests that her creative efforts in outer life may open the way to a creative solution to her inner conflict. Through withstanding the torments of initiation she may find an expression for passion that remains unaddressed in her marriage. Rather than running away to find an outlet for her passion, the dream suggests that she discover passion through artistic expression. In this case the symbol emerges while watching and understanding dreams. Kelly, like Lee and countless others, battles anxiety and depression, often struggling between the relief she experiences through medication and a desire to live the tension without pharmaceutical intervention . Again, "restlessness begets . . . soul-sickness," often preventing her from embracing a vitality trapped in the cave where opposites carry on their perpetual skirmish (Jung 1934b, par. 815).

Summary

The time of initiatory crisis has a number of components, each with its own unique profundity. The interconnection, overlapping, and coincidence of these phases present a tedious challenge to discern just what the process requires for continued flow and optimal growth.

Just as one answers the call, already rooted in throes of unsolvable conflict, the situation demands a sacrifice. Even in cases where a vocation rather than an occupation has materialized in the first half of life, one remains aware of unlived life, those parts of the personality relinquished, that is, sacrificed, when adolescent crisis demanded the answering of the call into adulthood and all the challenges inherent in taking responsibility for one's life. I know a young minister whose wife has left the marriage because she did not understand the depths of his devotion to the ministry and to continued study of theology and philosophy. Now realizing he must continue to answer his calling through a postgraduate discipline, he faces criticism of many family members because his study will take him away from the city in which he and his former wife share custody of their young son. His inner imperative now requires a restructuring of many lives. In the words of Jung quoted above, one is held captive by the daemon and is not free.

Sacrifice culminates in crisis, imaged by a metaphorical torture chamber where inner images of skinning, boiling, disembowelment, and so on, create pressure forceful enough to exact a turning point wherein re-membering may commence. Daily life feels unclear while an initiating ego, focused on an attempt to discover a path forward, experiences liminality, characterized by the acute loss of familiar connections with routine tasks.

Sacrifice, in turn, commands a number of typical processes, each difficult to delineate in the realm of psyche. Motifs of traditional initiation ritual provide a blueprint of events that articulates the flow. First, a paradoxical passage challenges the initiate's resolution to answer the call. Negotiating this passage means the novice sets aside rationality and ambition without discarding them and moves into a chamber of solitude, represented by images such as a cave, a monastery (which may rest at the top of a mountain), a forest, the belly of the beast, or the bottom of the sea, where unconscious images and their desires come into view. Moving toward a chamber of solitude compels the initiate to embark upon a perilous journey in deference to the one(s) who calls. In the place beyond the paradoxical passage, one's conscious strivings, the experience Eliade refers to as "the universe of daily life," must become very small, focused on fundamental things: food, hygiene, rest, and simple vigilance.

Finally the acolyte reaches the initiation chamber of the cave where real torture begins. Images of skinning, boiling in a cauldron, disembowelment, dismemberment, and complete reduction to a skeleton dominate the imagination. Psychologically, all ego attitudes and value systems come under scrutiny: suspended, sacrificed, and separated into component parts so that consciousness may entertain psychic messages and images previously unknown, unexplored. Ordinary life hangs in the balance while the individual minimizes the tempo of outer life and remains devoted to the inquiry through creative pursuits such as writing down dreams, engaging in active imagination, and composing reflective responses to the imaginal material, as well as endeavoring to express the images through artistic media.

One step into the habits that relieve the tension can contaminate the process and cause even more discomfort and delay. Like crawling through a cave tunnel, one must remain focused on reaching the inner chamber. Finding language that can help to discern and articulate the meaning imbedded in symbol can make the difference between new life and failure. Jung noticed that often during crisis, a patient's tenacious striving would falter, weakening the courage to continue, interrupting devotion to the soul, and testing faith in the spirit of life. A frenzied retreat would result, one that he referred to as "regressive restoration of the persona." If short-lived, this backward movement could serve to restore the patient's determination and strength to stay the course.

Andrew

Andrew, introduced earlier (p. 35), experienced just such a backward movement. Thinking he could manage his former addictive lifestyle in a different way, he stepped slowly back into it. In very little time he found himself in the old familiar underworld of compulsive obsession. Since he also had adopted an attitude of reflection and awareness toward himself, in outer life as well as inner imaginal life, Andrew realized in a short while that he had started to miss the joys of bike rides on sunny days and the excitement of working out the challenges of various creative projects looming on the horizon. Upon his decision to reenter the initiatory task, Andrew had the following dream:

> *I am back at Harvard, and this is the first day of school. My first class is calculus, and I'm late but I manage to get there. The class has started, and I see that the instructor is Charlotte from the TV series, Sex and the City. Rather than teaching calculus, however, she is showing a film. I can't remember exact details but recall the film showing a beautiful underwater world, flowing with color and serenity. I feel drawn to Charlotte because I happen to know that even though her character in the show is conservative, serious, and a bit naïve, in outer life she struggles with alcoholism. I perceive also that she has gotten past the addiction in order to teach calculus at Harvard. She represents someone who has confronted addiction and fought her way out of it. Unlike my previous experiences at Harvard, I resolve to attend classes, prepare for exams, read, and study for the joy of learning and discovering the many mysteries of life. Later in the dream, I am marrying Charlotte.*

Andrew reported that upon awakening from the dream the thought came to him: "This is the more mature you." His dreamer quickly responded to the awakening awareness that his addiction had once again captured him, emphasizing the necessity of his resolve to leave it alone. His dreamer anticipated a complete and successful initiation of the new life of wonder, discovery, and creativity that seemed ready to emerge. At once startling, aesthetic, and hopeful, the dream gave Andrew a renewed sense of life's inherent charm and natural erotic quality.

Through the awareness gained from following dreams and respecting their messages, Andrew felt his newfound joy of life slipping, and he quickly became resolved to continue forward through the changes he had inaugurated. However, if an individual has held too long to a familiar but depleted identification with the former patterns, accomplishments, and perspectives, the delicate thread of advance may break and the novitiate may be hurled back into the flat, grey, meaningless existence and painful suffering where the descent commenced. This could plunge a depleted ego into the soul's intent, where the call continues its wistful beckoning. Such backtracking into identification with a depleted persona fosters an interlude of discouragement and fear, which prolongs the agony by obscuring the core self in sackcloth, thereby preventing even a shred of healing. As Jung postulates in his paper explaining such a regressive reinstatement of previous patterns of behavior, "only what is really oneself has the power to heal" (Jung 1935, par. 258).

3

Living the Cure

Out of the memory, and within the memory,
the soul then pours forth its wealth of images—
of visions envisioning the soul itself.
—HEIDEGGER, WHAT IS CALLED THINKING?

Treatment of a neurosis is not a kind of psychological
water-cure, but a renewal of the personality, working
in every direction and penetrating every sphere of life.
—JUNG, "THE TRANSCENDENT FUNCTION"

An initiating shaman feels cured when soul-body reunites with physical body, rendering possible an ascension out of the cave. In the hero's journey, cure means return to the homeland, carrying the treasure of great value. Psychologically, it is the progression of psychic energy into outer life. Transformed by the trials of crisis, of torturous symbolic death, and merciful intervention by healing powers able to reconstruct and reconstitute the body, one reenters the net of relationships. If addressed consciously, constellation of an initiatory process can bring one into a larger sphere of life, a more complete expression of one's potential, a deeper understanding of the meaning of one's existence. During crisis, a symbol emerges which synthesizes unconscious potentials with conscious striving; this reconciling image brings meaning to the ordeal of transition and loss. Jung contends that transformation "is achieved by means of the symbol" (Jung 1948a, par. 113). A form of marriage occurs within the psyche when consciousness and the unconscious become familiar with one another and form an alliance that fertilizes the entire individual to live life differently. When the alliance, through ongoing relationship, develops a dynamic intimacy an individual lives in deference to the commands of the inner alliance such that something

59

new and creative makes itself known in the world. Jung referred to this marriage from within as *coniunctio*, a word which describes *coincidentia oppositorum*, or a union of opposites. At the pinnacle of initiation, just such an alliance occurs which in turn produces a symbol with strong and powerful influence on the initiate, a symbol kaleidoscopic enough to imbue the entire struggle with meaning and flood the individual with psychic energy.

Does the story of suffering end here? The initiate emerges from the ordeal with an adamantine body and an ally or guide that mediates communication with heaven and hell and "lives happily ever after." Of course we know that happiness is like a butterfly fluttering through the garden, momentarily visiting, then off again, or like a bee tasting sweet nectar from each blossom in a field of wildflowers. So if happiness never lingers, just what is the cure? Rebirth into a new perspective through which one reenters the world does not mean an end to suffering. It does not mean answers to all the Socratic questions. It does not mean an end to loss and sickness and longing. I might even be challenged to ask, "Does cure exist?"

My first impulse might be to answer a simple no. But then Jung's often-quoted characterization of psychoneurosis echoes in my mind: "the suffering of a soul which has not discovered its meaning" (Jung 1932, par. 497). Here the implication seems clear. Neurosis, that is, the illness ceases as soon as the suffering soul discovers meaning. And since body and soul, through enduring the initiatory trial with the wonder of a child, the critique of an adult, and the submission of a devotee, receive a reconciling and guiding symbol imbued with meaning, the neurosis finds a cure. Continuing to the end of the paragraph, however, brings me back to the question:

> But all creativeness in the realm of the spirit as well as every psychic advance of man arises from the suffering of the soul, and the cause of the suffering is spiritual stagnation, or psychic sterility. (Ibid., par. 497)

Here I might conclude that the suffering soul engenders a perpetually creative trajectory that allays psycho-spiritual torpor. And in that case my first impulse is correct: there is no cure. Then I must retire to poetry and along with poet and songwriter Leonard Cohen, lament in lyrical simplicity, "There ain't no cure for love," or life. Not only is there no cure, but everything seems to depend on the everlasting lack of cure. Recollecting Jung's characterization of the medicine man quoted in chapter 1 (p. 6), wherein he elevates to mythological truth the fact that "the wounded wounder is the agent of healing" and that the sufferer takes away suffering, brings the issue again to a conclusion that healing means suffering (Jung 1954b, par. 457). There is no cure in the traditional sense, at least not in the tradition dating, according to Barnhart, back to about 1380 when the word *cure* first described restoration to health. In the ancient sense, however, the Latin *cūra* means care, heed, charge, concern, attention, implying an ongoing relationship, a devotion to the malady (Barnhart 1995, 179). Amid disappointment that no once-for-all cure exists, one consolation remains: neurotic destitution falls away, like dust from a beaten carpet, when the new body emerges. Consciousness feels supported by presence, power, meaning.

A remarkable dream imaged the intervention of healing spirits at the culmination point of my own crisis when outer life had reached an almost unbearable feeling of hopelessness:

> *I am outside on a beach. Suddenly there is a mysterious spark from a mostly clear sky and out of it a body falls and is taken on board a small boat for treatment. Her skin has a beautiful pearlescent glow, but something of the masculine dwells within. The injury is very serious, but an attitude of healing prevails. I feel a profound sense of opening, like my way has been cleared by the spark.*

My analyst helped me to understand the dream as anticipation of a major shift in my being. Treatment on the boat images consecration of the subtle (pearlescent) body, paralleling shamanic motifs of re-memberment by spiritual beings or ancestors. At the time of this dream the sense of opening experienced by the dream ego eluded me, the waking ego. I felt abandoned, alone, even utterly hopeless at times. The dream provided a suggestion echoed by my analyst, a promise of the possibility of cure. My waiting and my struggle to attend to the necessities of life received a directive which molded the determination to survive, to attend to my professional life and take care of my body, while submitting myself to the mystery of spiritual intervention. Jung noticed the same sort of healing process in his clients and explains:

> It is as though, at the climax of the illness, the destructive powers were converted into healing forces. This is brought about by the archetypes awaking to independent life and taking over the guidance of the psychic personality, thus supplanting the ego with its futile willing and striving.

As a religious-minded person would say: guidance has come from God.
(Jung 1932, par. 534)

A. P. Elkin reports a visionary experience of the Australian shaman
that images the change from destruction to a more sublime construction
or healing: totemic spirits "kill," then cut the initiate from neck to groin
so as to extract all the organs. The same entities then insert materials
considered by the community to carry numinous qualities, for example,
quartz crystals (Elkin 1994, 21). Notice the provocative image of the
soul-body enduring painful torture and then rendered immaculate by
spiritual intervention. Quartz crystals evoke the same sense of glow as
the pearlescence in my dream and image the adamantine quality mentioned in chapter 2 (p. 47–48). Also, in concert with Jung's statement, the
spirits that kill also provide the magical substance, that is, "the destructive powers were converted into healing forces" (1932, par. 534). During
the most critical time magic is aroused, releasing the elixir or transformative substance that renders an initiating shaman capable of taking the
illnesses of others into the healer's body and transforming them.

The soft glow of quartz crystals emphasizes a change in the body itself, the very ground of one's being. The image of crystals becomes a
transformative symbol. But how, one might ask, does an individual in
the modern world who has chosen to answer a call and suffer the tension of conflict and the trauma of crisis experience the physical impact
of the reconciling symbol? I have noticed that clients change their hair-
style, their manner of dress, or make even more permanent changes like
acquiring their first tattoo.

Quinn

Quinn, a very reflective, accomplished, and exacting man, after much
devotion to his initiatory process, decided to have his reconciling symbol inked on his chest over the area of his heart. He conscientiously
channeled the pain into the release of sadness experienced in childhood
around which sexual repression had later gathered. He realized that the
emergent symbol provided the image of passion through which sexual
expression could flow in a full spectrum of experience.

For changes in the body in response to spiritual development, the
Eastern kundalini experience provides the most time-honored examples. Various tantric systems define a subtle body which dwells within
the physical body. Centers of energy define this subtle body and respond

to various yogic practices. These practices combine meditation, breath work, and body postures as well as dietary observances. The various practices activate the energy centers causing certain individuals to experience what yogis refer to as a "kundalini awakening."

Most of the time the kundalini releases in a beautiful array of images and feelings of euphoria. However, some individuals who engage in yogic practice experience traumatic physical episodes as a result of the release of kundalini energy. Western doctors often have puzzled over unexplained symptoms and mysterious medical emergencies that seem to have no logical connection to physical indicators of the episode. Lee Sannella, a psychiatrist and ophthalmologist, published a book in 1976 entitled *Kundalini: Psychosis or Transcendence?* in which thirteen cases of kundalini experience are reported. He explains the physical symptoms that manifest as the kundalini releases, as well as his struggle to compile an accurate diagnosis. He attempted to distinguish between psychosis and physical illness as opposed to a kundalini awakening process. Sannella attributes symptoms such as short-term partial paralysis to overwhelming fear of the process experienced by certain individuals. In his work with these patients he noticed that the fear would subside in the presence of explanation and emotional support. It seems that naïve Westerners who engage in frequent and regular yogic practices, especially meditation, may experience the unexpected release of kundalini energy as an incident that frightens and dis-integrates them from within.

On a more positive note, Sannella compares a medical description of the experience with that of the birth experience, revealing a striking similarity. Spiritual rebirth emerges from traumatic muscular spasms; sharp pains surge from the feet, up the legs, back, and neck, and finally into the head, which feels as if it will burst just before a radiance or "sunburst" floods the entire being. Sannella adopts the phrase "psycho-spiritual transformation" to describe the painful rebirth process (Sannella 1976, 1). His description of kundalini carries all of the aspects of initiation, with the individual realizing a profound sense of oneness that remains and informs life. A spirit of nondual awareness informs the attitude, and individuals experience surges of creativity, an empathy with nature, and a sense of the sacred never before noticed. Nondual awareness brings one into an experience of complete reality that contains all the ambiguities present in our human condition and allows an underlying unity to support decisions, human relationships, ideas, and perceptions of waking consciousness. Jung adopted a Latin term first suggested by the pre-Socratic Greek philosopher Heraclitus: *coincidentia opposi-*

torum. Meaning coincidence or unity of opposites, he used the term to describe the tense cohabitation of all contradictions, a quality of the Self which seeks to embrace and contain the ego. In order to attain the slightest awareness of the most powerful and benevolent component of existence, the ego must submit to tolerant contemplation of the inherent ambiguity of all life.

Gopi Krishna, a yogi from India, has written extensively about his very traumatic kundalini awakening. He believes that the occurrence of these experiences will increase as humans become more spiritually mature. He refers to this collective phenomenon as "spiritual evolution." In his book *Kundalini: The Evolutionary Energy in Man*, he offers a biographical journal of the uncommonly traumatic awakening of the powerful and mysterious energy of kundalini. Krishna goes so far as to suggest that the well-being of humankind depends on acknowledgment and development of this engendering mechanism perpetually active through an organic central core of the body. Awareness of the energy, seemingly awakened, remains on one hand a mysterious gift, not unlike experiences described by mystics, saints, and others who experience an interruption of consciousness that feels tremendously ecstatic. On the other hand it seems that increasing numbers of common individuals report experiences of the awakening of kundalini, the overwhelming majority of whom have engaged in some litany of voluntary and regular devotional practice such as meditation, yoga, tantra, or other inwardly focused movement traditions.

Predating the dream of my subtle body undergoing healing by benevolent spirit doctors, I experienced a definite change in body awareness. Prefaced by a period of lower back pain and spontaneous jerks in the midsection of my body, I noticed a somewhat electrical, vibrating radiance that one day pervaded my entire body, characterized by an upward flow. At that time I was preparing to teach a course at the Jung Center in Houston, pivoting on Jung's lectures on kundalini yoga and including an inquiry into the reported occurrences of kundalini experience. Synchronistically, the study provided valuable insight into my own experience. Each kundalini experience presents differently, leaving me no rational certainty as to what abounds through my body; however, the sensation of an upsurge of energy remains with me to this day, a constant reminder of the pearlescent subtle body that lives in me. Like Anne Sexton, I feel "untamable, eternal" love, together with reverence and humility toward the mysterious other making itself known in and through me. The perpetual soft flow also brings to mind St. Paul's revelation to the Galatians (2:20): "I live no longer; not I, but God lives in me." I regard it as a sacred indwelling that carries me along when my will falters, even fails. The sensation remains ineffable; however, some people seem to see it. Total strangers periodically stop to tell me about my "glow."

Transformed during the excruciating crisis of initiation, the new body marks an expanded awareness which informs every thought, decision, reaction, idea, expression, and almost every intentional movement. Robed with an invisible but perceptible adamantine presence, the new eyes seem to reflect and transmit light; the outer body seems lighter, mannerisms take on an open, hospitable quality. More important, one's being has achieved the adamantine quality of unbreakable integrity. The initiate has achieved a turning point whereby daemonic forces have shifted, through grace, into beneficent influences. Continuing to dwell in the containing space while torn to shreds in the struggle has bestowed upon the sufferer the power to maintain relationship with these paradoxical forces. Authorities which officiated the suffering ego and symbolically cut open the sacrificed body herald from the same divinity that in turn configures a new body and inserts the magical crystals. Jung summarizes the dual aspects of God revealed in the Revelation of John in the Christian New Testament:

> God has a terrible double aspect: a sea of grace is met by a seething lake of fire, and the light of love glows with a fierce dark heat. (Jung 1952a, par. 733)

Precisely this paradoxical quality tortures the initiate in the cave and then snatches essence out of the ego's defeat. An initiate reduced to the very seed of essence braves spiritual crisis contingent upon entering a paradox as tremendous as a "sea of grace" and a "lake of fire." According to Eliade, emerging from spiritual crisis culminating in initiatory death demands awareness of the religious significance resting at the crux of the experience. An initiate's sufferings give rise to the attainment of shaman status only through the realization of meaning amid suffering, thereby embracing the pain as a necessity in the creative struggle, like a woman in the throes of labor. Recognizing the meaning establishes "mystical transfiguration." Integration of the shaman's new personality relies on a curing (Eliade 1958, 91).

The culmination of my own crisis hung by a thread to spiritual wisdom that carried religious significance for cultures far outside my own. Yet my soul reached back to the very dawn of human ecstatic experience, shamanism, before I found a net of meaning that saved my life. It was then that I realized a cure. Through losing a life that had exhausted its purpose and integrating a new way of understanding life and of living in the world I feel a sense of peaceful acceptance of the situation and find meaning amid the agony of loss.

I continue to embody an orphaned soul, feeling no real connection to a family or a religious system, suffering in the solitude of a hard-won perspective like the shaman who must make his dwelling on the outskirts of the community. The ancient doll in my dream (p. xiii) seems to connect with the idea of orphan: left behind, forgotten in the basement of a distant world, waiting to be discovered. The man in the passenger's seat, as spirit guide or shamanic ancestor, inspires me with curiosity and the courage to peer inside the doll. A later dream offers a progressive development of the image of orphan as well as the dual aspect of God described by Jung in the above quote.

> I am handed a baby. He speaks clearly and with wisdom. I know he is with me for a reason. I feel a sacred responsibility. The scene changes a bit. People are on a pilgrimage and boarding a train. They are fighting some force of evil that periodically claims someone. I am not afraid of the force, but I have no power to prevent the suffering and loss; I can only dissuade the evil by my presence. At some point a man with blonde disheveled hair and a timeless, beautiful face bonds with me. I am aware that he is the baby, now a man. I was somehow separated from the baby but now understand that the estrangement was necessary so that he could become my companion. The scene changes again, and I am alone, walking along a remote road. I encounter a giant mound of rock moving very slowly just above the ground as though it is sitting on a huge trailer being pulled by an invisible force. I watch as it lights up as if ignited by a fire within. In seconds the mound glows like hot coals. I am aware that there is a secret passage for me to enter a chamber where the blonde man dwells.

An orphaned baby has developed into companion, a gift of grace; however, the adult man dwells at the center of fire. The dream ego will meet her divine guide if she can find the secret passage. This dream offers hope for the one who is called to dissuade evil by her presence, and also for the one who longs for an intense bond. I often feel this sort of calling in relation to clients. I can do nothing about their suffering; however, a mystery seems to dwell in the act of listening, encouraging, and questioning and by being an engaged presence.

Rolling Thunder's pronouncement (p. 4) that the power must be used suggests something beyond peaceful acceptance. That the power must be used suggests integration of some knowledge into one's attitude or mode of existence. What directive remains to a life altered by an ordeal that leaves one feeling alienated and out of touch with a modern society vibrating with rapidly changing generations of cell phones, iPods, tablets, computers, energy sources, politics, and deeper unknowns of physical knowledge? How, in such a world, does one participate in the mystery discovered through repetitions of intense dissolution? Rolling Thunder's little three-letter word, *use*, suggests that a respectable, humble sharing must ensue. Such an expression emerges in a kaleidoscope of forms, depending on the particular gifts and impulses of a given individual. The pitfall lies in neglecting the ideas for creative expression, allowing the new energy gained through all the torture of initiatory trial to dissipate. Cure does not exist without maintaining a relationship to the experience. One might write a book or a computer program, paint on canvas or on a wall, dance on stage or under the full moon, speak words of inspiration to the multitude or to one sad heart.

The shaman's contribution rests in the ecstatic experience. Eliade observed that ecstatic experience includes many facets and exists in concert with the human condition, informing and integrating the human journey of attaining consciousness of one's individual style of being in the world (1991, 100–101). Eliade here seems to suggest that using the power means integrating the power, which depends on maintaining a perpetual relationship to inner psychic life through an ongoing and active awareness and imagination, that is, living in harmony with the ecstatic experience. In the twenty-first century any man or woman has the opportunity to bring into one's life the experience of a psychic enactment that will inevitably arrive in concert with a feeling that life has lost its meaning. Due to the pioneering work of Sigmund Freud and Carl Jung, modern individuals may develop and expand their awareness through ongoing attention to dreams, devotion to active imagination, and a dynamic curiosity in response to synchronicity, thereupon contributing to life with compassion and wisdom. In *Such Stuff As Dreams Are Made On*, Helen Luke offers her description of the experience of ecstasy as it permeates the common tasks of everyday life. As a "state of being outside the ego," Luke maintains that ecstasy enkindles liberation from the insistence of the ego's agenda, conducted by grasping, and transports one into an awareness of unity beyond ego desires, where joie de vivre brings together opposites of neither (desire nor emptiness of desire) and both (Luke 2000, 31).

Healing in the shamanic tradition requires contact with ancestors, the divine source of soul, memory, and creation—a contact made possible through imagination, ecstasy, and entertaining the mystery. The shaman seeks and cultivates relationship with imaginal figures who guide him into and around other areas of experience which is seasoned with sound, vision, and bodily sensations. Flights into imagination comprise intentional journeys into world and underworld. If, through imagination, one contacts the divine, then it seems to follow that it is just this contact that accomplishes healing. One has "seen the light," and one must integrate—or use—the inner situation now made clear.

The dice contained in the homunculus figure in my dream (p. xiii) point to fate, to that which is inevitable, to the sacrifice inherent in discovery. Cooper's encyclopedia of symbols connects dice with Christ's passion (1978, 51). Jesus said, "Now is my soul troubled; and what shall I say? Father, save me from this hour: but for this cause came I unto this hour" (John 12:27). For my part, I answered a call that is still calling. Jesus sacrificed his connection to the earthly plane and attained a higher level of being. The shaman sacrifices conventional connection to society and attains a sacred existence. I sacrificed life as I knew it, which pales in comparison, but it was my sacrifice given my humble existence and its limitations. Through enduring the loss and bowing before the greater purpose that brought me to it, I attained greater awareness. I do not and cannot offer my clients healing per se; I can only facilitate a more comprehensive sense of their place in the world, their life's meaning, and their creative destiny.

One might conclude that contact with the ancestor, the god, the guide, ally, or wise one means the beginning of suffering. These figures, as symbols, connect unconscious strivings with conscious talents, interests, and endeavors, often achieving a creative life of which the initiate could have never previously conceived. All unnecessary ego attachments, however, must fall away, and in this falling away lies the greatest suffering: the suffering that accompanies loss. But then creative suffering ensues, that is, anyone caught up in the inspiration of creative expression suffers. Relating to the image thus received, like living a life of service, demands enormous commitment, devotion, endurance, intimacy, and loyalty. In turn, gifts issuing from devotion to one's unique living symbol exact rewards every bit as great as the sacrifice: inspiration, creativity, companionship, exuberance, love, an inner fountain of youth.

Eliade explains the process of symbol making by archaic people:

> Objects or acts acquire a value, and in so doing become real, because they participate, after one fashion or another, in a reality that transcends them. Among countless stones, one stone becomes sacred—and hence instantly becomes saturated with being—because it constitutes a hierophany, or possesses mana, or again because it commemorates a mythical act, and so on. The object appears as the receptacle of an exterior force that differentiates it from its milieu and gives it meaning and value. (1954, 3–4)

A dream image becomes real in just the same way. Out of a perpetual procession of dreams one image or sequence catches the eye of consciousness and follows the dreamer into waking and wondering, often shaken by curiosity, fear, or attraction, that is, the image transmits numinosity. For myself, the serpent arrived in a dream, following an early childhood experience of encountering the poisonous strike, the pain, the acute crippling, and most of all, the trauma of an unseen instant whereby one's life changes. This is the ultimate meaning of the serpent: change. Through innumerable dreams, the serpent has become my totem, ally, and personal symbol. It seems to insist that I regularly shed my skin, that I dwell below the surface of collective convention while participating in that collective, all the while paying homage to occult mysteries such as initiation. The serpent also brought me to the study of shamanism by way of my analysts, independently and regularly, as they both amplified serpents in my dreams with shamanic motifs. Kundalini yoga images the inner energy moving upward as a serpent coiled three and a half times around the base of the spine until awakened, at which time it moves up through the centers of energy called chakras.

Consecration, or lifting to a place of spiritual meaning, of the numinous personal symbol, releases a wealth of psychic energy which manifests in an enlarged personality, a new ego attitude, informed by integration of consciousness with unconscious contents. For such an attitude Jung adopted the term *transcendent function*, an attitude that interlaces essentials of ego consciousness with powerful unconscious contents, thereby informing a revitalized consciousness. The shamanic initiate who enters the cave through the tortuous and narrow passage, imaged by the serpent's body, in turn discovers a cosmic portal to another reality with the aid of the sanctification of the symbol; tortuous underground body of the serpent becomes the feathered serpent, for instance, a symbol of ascent (Ryan 2002, 183). The most well-known feathered serpent, the Aztec Quetzalcoatl, is associated with self-reflection and with the morning star. One reaches the morning star only through surviving the night sea journey, a descent in order to reach the clarity of light and wisdom of reflection.

Symbol making and dedication of the symbol depend on a process of enantiodromia which converts disturbing—even traumatic—imaginal experience to its opposite; the descent becomes the way to ascent. The snake that bit me became a guide into and through unconscious realities: oceans, caverns, mansions, ungrounded heavens and fiery hells, towers and basements, forests and cities, distant futures and dark pasts. Symbols transform through endurance of initiation, and in so doing, unveil the mystery of one transforming oneself through a courageous engagement with inner images, imperatives, and initiatives; one enters into the potentiality of both redeemer and redeemed (Ryan 2002, 90).

Doran

Doran, introduced earlier, found strength in her endeavors to articulate meaning brought by a wealth of synchronicity and forged ahead into many creative projects. A dream reported just before her decision to begin studies at Pacifica Graduate Institute anticipated release of the psychic energy usurped by tensions arising out of disturbing discoveries of events surrounding her father's emotional illness.

> *I awake with a smile and relive a dreamlike, fleeting memory—"Yes, it really was a dream," I tell myself. This dream is not in a linear timely sequence of vivid scenes and is difficult to pin down. I see two little bluebirds fluttering toward me, and they alighted on a triangle, each one on opposing corners. The triangle is an open, equilateral form. The feeling I had from this dream was immense blessing. I have experienced a revealed truth.*

Birds often signal release of psychic energy. In the Mayan tradition one finds the Celestial Bird sitting atop the World Tree (Ryan 2002, 162). Jung says, "The tree with the bird stands for the opus and its consummation" (Jung 1954c, par. 415). Winged creatures in general form a "symbol of ascent and portend the turning of consciousness at the nadir of . . . experience which will lift [the shaman] to a higher awareness" (Ryan

2002, 235). Blue, also "the color of air and sky, is most readily used for depicting spiritual contents" (Jung 1954a, par. 414n), and the bird as redeeming figure, a symbol for soul in ancient Egypt (Jung 1952c, par. 845), points to the fact that Doran did in fact experience a revealed truth. The triangle is the shape of the Greek letter delta, which in the system of calculus denotes change. It quite appropriately symbolizes the transcendent function—a third point that rises above two opposing points, yet retaining substance from each of them and facilitating relationship between them.

Connecting with ancestors often means connecting with ancient myth (in my own story, through the symbol of serpent) that carries meaning for an individual's experience, gifts, and limitations. However, Doran's case provides a provocative example of literally exploring and understanding her own recent ancestral story, which began to unfold for her upon the death of her father. She neither set her emotions aside nor brought them along in her systematic research effort. While Doran was pouring through courthouse records, trying to solve the mystery of a sudden inexplicable sale of her father's beloved property she also worked in creative space, below the mundane exploration at the courthouse, to bring the pieces together in a film and art exhibit engendered by walking the land and reading journals left by her father as well as his mother. Her analysis took on the character of an artist's workshop wherein Doran brought images and memories and synchronicities and placed them within a frame of meaning. After graduating from the institute, Doran took up a renewed participation in the world. She radiates a sense of well-being, of confidence, of belonging. Her story provides an evocative variation of Rolling Thunder's edict that one must use the energy.

Using the gift of healing gained by the shaman involves integrating instinctive animal qualities apprehended through imaginative relationship with theriomorphic spirit guides. Anthropologists who have studied Chauvet Cave in France surmise a symbolic relationship between animals and humans, especially the bear. Ancient cultures found a parallel between shaman and bear—"both of them considered as mediators between the human community and the spirit world" (Bahn 2003, 203–204). In one depiction, ninety-two palm impressions form the image of a large herbivore. Does this image mean a placing of hands on the animal figure, or does it mean something far more complicated? Bahn suggests that by forming the body of the animal using an essential human feature like the hand demonstrates a "merged perception" between human and bear (ibid.). Heidegger reasons that the human hand differs from grasping organs of other creatures in that it has a unique ability to design and to create handicraft, which requires imaginative thought processes (1968, 16). Further, the hands together forming one hand seem to transport an individual into a oneness with an ineffable unity. Does our knowledge of the most primal communities imply that humans have always instinctively and imaginatively connected with a meaning that shrinks from view yet maintains tremendous closeness? Jung borrowed a term from Lucien Lévy-Bruhl, *participation mystique*, whereby relationships with objects become less individual and more imbued with a partial identification. Human hands forming the image of bear evoke just such a relationship, one which transmits powerful bear qualities into human imagination, thereby protecting the shaman from harmful influences in the spirit world.

The Mayan glyph translated as "way" depicts a king's face half covered with an animal pelt. It carries a fourfold meaning: to transform, to dream, the animal spirit guide, and the shaman himself. Initiation forges a pathway to healing, transformation, and renewal, to power within dream, to companionship with instinctual awareness, to appeasement of spiritual imperative through shamanizing: the healing practice of the shaman (Ryan 2002, 106). Other members of the tribe, not unlike our current social establishment, often view these inner relationships as mystical and potentially dangerous. However, tribal members realize that the shaman has survived death and now communicates with qualities that consecrate a hands-on touch (a dream, a vision, a dance) so that healing transpires. The shaman has acquired mana, a power both essential and out of the ordinary. Surviving the torture of dismemberment, disembowelment, or dissolution (boiling) has brought the initiate into contact with existential essence wherein the foundational energy of life, the soul, the Self, resides. Jung understood mana, or the mysterious nature of the shaman's healing power, in terms of psychic energy. As a result of initiation an exceptional energy permeates the consecrated shaman's being, impregnating the individual with an ineffable fecundity, an exceptionally powerful energy which manifests through an array of personal stimuli that provoke expression (Jung 1948a, par. 126).

Encountering Essence

We have learnt that there are spiritual processes of transformation in the psyche which underlie, for example, the well-known initiation rites of primitive peoples and the states induced by the practice of yoga. (Jung 1934a, par. 688)

Essence. That which lies *in potencia*, obscured by ore that appears unattractive, rough, dull, earthen, silent. Perhaps its rough and earthen nature receives another layer of obscurity fashioned by the human milieu, this time informed by a quality of illusion: designer costume, sculptured nails, big hair, jewelry, makeup, and addiction to societal fictions. Essence glistens beneath it all, but remains incognito, unseen, unexpressed, unmined, and/or forgotten. It seems that only through inquiry, observation, insight, penetrating the ore, the outer wrapping, through remembering that which may never have stirred in consciousness, does one approach essence. Shamanic tradition culminates in stripping the initiate to the bone, a symbol of exposing essence, truth, power, destiny of the individual. How does one remember the forgotten, discover one's essence, obtain the golden key that unlocks the hidden and reveals truth? Mining the treasures of a forgotten soul requires devotion, introspection, willingness to sacrifice a confining persona, like a snake sheds its skin. My dream of being skinned alive, through punishment for a crime against the state (or the foundation of things) suggested that destiny had taken charge (p. xx). I had clung too long to a situation that had been lived to the breaking point.

Revolution, turning around, necessarily involves war. That is, a spiritual war against everything one has known to be true. It involves ruthless discernment, examination rather than acceptance, doubt rather than blind faith. It involves enduring the terror of one's own demons as well as cultivating the guidance of one's angels, and revolution together with redemption lies at the core of initiation. Revolution and transformation associate with each other through meaning. Jung elaborates the idea of being pierced by one's own arrow:

> As we know that the arrow is a libido-symbol, the meaning of this "piercing" is clear: it is the act of union with oneself, a sort of self-fertilization, and also a self-violation, a self-murder. (Jung 1952b, par. 447)

A gulf of reflection, awareness, and courage, echoing a sacred "Yes!" to the uncertainty of transition and thus to life itself, unfolds upon a stage of suffering. Like institutionally conditioned convicts, however, many cling to whatever feels familiar and safe even though it means a life of repetition, boredom, and confinement, resisting release of the very inspiration that brought the person into existence.

Plato's cave analogy, interpreted by Heidegger in his lectures on the essence of truth, first expostulates a failed attempt at freeing the prisoner from the cave:

> There in the cave, turned to the shadows, he has no inkling of what will happen when he must see in the light; he has no pain in his eyes, and above all, there amidst the shadows he moves within that which he is capable of, which demands no great effort of him, and happens of its own accord so to speak. There amidst the shadows, in his shackles, he finds his familiar ground, where no exertion is required, where he is unhindered, where nothing recoils upon him, where there is no confusion, and where everyone is in agreement. (Heidegger 2002, 27)

Confrontation with the annihilator, fear, often requires torturous isolation, seemingly far from "familiar ground." Heidegger asserts that "liberation is only genuine when he who is liberated thereby becomes free for himself, i.e., comes to stand in the ground of his essence" (Heidegger 2002, 28). The ground of one's essence offers a solitary abode populated only by the presence of that to which one devotes the opus.

Hilda

Shortly after entering analysis, Hilda decided to enlist her husband to help her finish a cottage on their property so that she could start a Reiki practice. One day on her way back to the main house after working most of the day on the cottage, Hilda had a vision of a woman's foot. She described it as large and earthy, one that had seldom worn shoes, enabling her to enjoy the feeling of earth or grass on her bare soles. The foot reminded Hilda of a popular mystic artist with whom she had made acquaintance recently. This vision carried a power far beyond its natural simplicity. The image of such an intentional and strong foot seemingly rooted with every step formed the foundation of Hilda's analysis, providing an anchor for her work. She learned that whenever she found herself in an episode of anxiety and depression she could envision the strong foot, the mystical grounding that stood at the essence of her being.

Hilda learned to practice active imagination, often connecting with her wise figures when outer life constellated her complexes and hurled her into the identity of a disheartened little girl constantly reprimanded and, at best, ignored. The guides of her imaginal space repeatedly put her through the tearing apart and remolding of initiatory dramas, always leaving Hilda in a state of an encouraged attitude toward life and the peace of mind that she would heal. In time she found the energy and the courage to pursue further certifications that would enhance her Reiki practice, which blossomed into a sanctuary where her identity felt completely transformed and valuable.

Let us return to the threads of initiation: apprehending the call, negotiating the crisis, and living the cure, with an emphasis on negotiating the crisis. Exploring the soul through imagination reveals the hidden, the secret, the unknown and unrevealed. Heidegger, in *The Essence of Truth* (2002), painstakingly postulates a philosophical justification for translating the Greek word for truth as "unhiddenness." The faculty of imagination connects conscious awareness to its divine source and unlocks, reveals, and brings one's unique personal truth into awareness.

How does a wounded healer, that is, a shaman accomplish the initiatory healing that endures the night sea journey? Through imagination, through devotion, and through an innocent foolishness, a childlike curiosity and courage. Heidegger, in his reflections on Nietzsche's *Thus Spoke Zarathustra*, asserts that "the destination toward which the one in transition is heading will only come to the fore in the transition itself" (Heidegger 1984, 220). The goal dwells in the unknowable future, perceptible only through imagination. Who would book passage on such a voyage? It goes against every fiber of reasonable pragmatism, yet willingness to entertain mystery brings an insurgence of hope to mingle amid one's suffering.

How does one explain such ineffable uncertainty to a wife whose marriage has long ago lost every shred of vitality ever available to it, who apprehends a call which may require that she trade her Mercedes for a used Volkswagen, her spending habits for artistic expression, and her McMansion for a two-room flat? The prospect of embracing a whimsical, self-nurturing freedom does seem curiously enticing to her, but she must tear herself free from the fear that she will not be able to negotiate the crisis of dramatic change, as well as the guilt inherent in abandoning her marriage. Yet she exists in a sea of anxiety, unexplained illnesses, boredom, hopelessness, and self-recrimination.

How does one answer a husband who must choose between wife and child, who both require the care of a father, and the calling of his soul's destiny? Even though his wife proves incapable of sustaining a mature partnering relationship, she expects him to remain on hand to carry the bulk of the responsibility in raising their son. He must wrestle through the dark night with every tradition he has learned to respect in order to remain true to his own soul and open himself to a creative solution to the problem which allows continued devotion to the imperative of his unique truth.

The wife characterized in the introduction to this book could be a husband, and the husband a wife. These human dilemmas repeat themselves time and again, always fundamentally the same, whether husband or wife, gay or straight. The analytical relationship ideally serves as a container for investigations into unanswered questions and conflicts amid life in the world and life of the soul, providing a sounding board and support for negotiating and enduring the crisis of decision, change, and solution, a floor for the dance, a canvas for the brush, a blank page for the pen, an ear that hears the dream.

However, our modern culture still often denigrates one's devotion to analysis as a sign of weakness, self-absorption, and wasted resources. Society piles guilt and shame upon those who seek support and guidance through relationship with a professional, creating added burdens for those who do seek analysis during spiritual crisis. A person seeking to understand the soul through rugged individualism risks falling into darkness with "no direction home," as singer-songwriter Bob Dylan put it.

Achieving a transcendent function of consciousness, a new attitude, resurrection from symbolic death, requires devotion and concentration throughout the preceding six steps. The process can be thwarted at any juncture, whereby one returns to the beginning. Every psychotherapist is familiar with the client who has been married several times to spouses who seem to replicate certain characteristics, and every addiction counselor has witnessed countless relapses just at the point where the recovering client seems stronger than ever. Whereas a traditional initiate had to complete the initiation ordeal or die, modern individuals must suffer a repeating motif until the symbol is integrated or until death puts a stop to the process, whichever comes first. Many years may escape during which a resistant ego refuses to accept the task of change or throughout which a particularly enigmatic symbol reveals its meaning to consciousness. *The Red Book* reveals Jung's discovery that the only reliable freedom, that is, inner freedom, requires sacrifice of one's visible success in favor of following oneself, obtaining self-knowledge, self-acceptance, and then embracing the torment of one's own way. Jung goes on to explain that inner freedom arises only through the symbol.

Repeated marriages or repeated dissatisfying jobs or chronic intoxication serve only as escape mechanisms while the symbol itself hides in the destruction, unspoken and unknown. When a client's marriage or significant relationship comes into question in the analytic container, often progress of the individual analysis stalls in deference to the issue at hand: the marriage and the spouse. I typically advise my client to take some time to reflect on what the spouse's presence in life has meant. Even if the relationship seems hopeless and needs to dissolve, premature flight could land the client squarely in the midst of another relationship that seems different but at its core presents the same issues and constellates the same complexes. Similarly, in a relationship with an employer: What has that position and that company meant? What has it taught? What opportunities have emerged, and has the situation provided all it can to the particular individual in question? Engaging in such a line of questioning continues and fertilizes the analysis, bringing added self-knowledge and confidence to the individual. But what happens when an individual neglects the often confrontational and severe task of exploring these meanings and takes a hasty flight out the door? In such a case marriages and job situations tend to take on a repetitive quality not unlike the cycle of addiction whereby an addict repeatedly seeks a feeling of well-being that proves false and temporary. Ego feels lost, fatigued, confused, and many people resort to addictions, whether socially acceptable or not, to assuage the tension and depression. Here again I observe that *a suffering soul is worse than a suffering body*.

Call may issue from a cry of tragedy which awakens a heroic nature. Answering requires submission to a quest to determine just what it is that one's soul may require. Endurance in the quest and devotion to an often tedious and irrational endeavor requires faith: not faith in an all-powerful god or in the wisdom of scripture obscured by too many layers of translation, but faith in oneself and in the personal divine ally that has never been known. Call exacts sacrifice and leads to crisis. However, only through sacrifice and subsequent crisis will the initiate ever attain a new realm of being and live with a transcendent function of consciousness, that is, "a movement out of the suspension between opposites, a living birth that leads to a new level of being, a new situation" (Jung 1958, par. 189), and herein lies the cure. The quest appears as a breakdown and may even be labeled as such. At the very point of feeling completely exhausted—decomposed, dissolved, dis-membered—the miracle comes in the form of a dream or a vision or an idea that puts everything back together.

Initiation successfully completed is followed by a ritual reentry into the tribal life to enact a different role: a vocation replete with the responsibilities of a shaman. In this way a constant dance develops between outer world and inner journey. Ego consciousness integrates experiences of a dream ego living a different existence that is somehow also the same existence: ambition more nearly resembles devotion, the quest for knowledge becomes experiencing gnosis, and instinct serves meaning. Doran answered a call which she also continues to answer. She has finished her master's degree and now lives with a renewed approach to her art through offering workshops and classes which incorporate the story of her exploration of the land of her father and the journey into her own soul. Each person mentioned in the foregoing chapters has found an outlet through creative activity for their mostly hard-won insights. Beatrice has earned a PhD in poetry. Al has renewed his energy for building a retreat for himself on rural land he inherited, where he hopes to find more time to devote to the crafting of his exquisite flutes. Kelly has leased an art studio where her creative passions find expression. She has also enrolled in a certificate program to study Jungian theory and philosophy, which provides a forum where her emotional and psychological insights find expression. Lee, almost forty at the time and with the help of an anonymous donor, conscientiously became pregnant and now has a beautiful little boy. Her devotion to his well-being led her to dissolve the relationship with her disturbed partner. These endeavors cost time, energy, and money with very little hope for future monetary profit. Our culture balks at such investments that promise little hope of return. Yet our souls continue the struggle to heal our lives, sending a questioning reply: How much am I worth?

4

Embodying Liberation

India affected me like a dream, for I was and remained in
search of myself, of the truth peculiar to myself.
—C. G. JUNG , MEMORIES, DREAMS, REFLECTIONS

Reexamining call, crisis, and cure, a few essential ideas bear repetition. Call announces a psychic drive toward renewal, that is, inner psychic enactment of the archetype of initiation, and may appear at any time in an individual's life. This is true even though previously described times of crisis remain important and predictable, such as adolescence, midlife, and retirement. Crisis follows on the heels of call whether one submits to the call or not. It is characterized by a time of confusion, seclusion, and/ or loss, culminating in symbolic death. Crisis carries within its chaos an image which, if fully negotiated (a process marked by discerning the message of the unconscious and envisioning its meaning for one's outer life), adumbrates a vehicle for carrying life energy back into consciousness and daily life. Cure, rather than a restoration of former security and comfort, means ongoing relationship to the symbol born out of crisis, a life of service and sacrifice in deference to the purpose which issues from the very core of one's being.

Nietzsche's *Zarathustra* epitomizes the ongoing practice of initiation requisite to psychic blossoming and the course of individuation. The book commences with Zarathustra having spent ten years in the mountains alone. "Here he enjoys his spirit and his solitude" (Nietzsche 1968, 121). Eventually he realizes a weariness has invaded his serenity and decides he must "go under," which means descending the mountain to share his wisdom bred in the clarity of stillness. On his way down he encounters an old monk in the woods who admonishes him: "You carried your ashes to the mountains; would you now carry your fire into the valleys? Do you not fear to be punished as an arsonist?"

(ibid., 122). Ignoring the warning, Zarathustra continues his descent with the intention of bringing something important to the world. Why must he proceed with a necessity to spread the fire rekindled through introversion? Recall the words of Rolling Thunder quoted in chapter 1 (p. 4) describing the imperative accompanying the awareness of a force that brought him through his own shamanic initiation: "a power which comes to you, which you have to honor, respect, and use; otherwise it can make you sick." What does it mean, then, to use the power? For Rolling Thunder it meant a life dedicated to the healing arts inherent in his position of tribal shaman. In general, it means understanding what heals you and then expressing it in the world in your own disciplined and creative way. The snake that bit me and then appeared in my dreams in a more sublime, spiritual form led me to the works of C. G. Jung, where I found my own cure and faced the challenge of living it. Just like the force residing with the old shaman, fire has only two avenues of being, one detrimental and destructive, one creative and beneficial. Cure as ongoing relationship with the wound means expression. It means sharing the gift even when the world accepts your gentle flame with limited capacity for genuinely receiving it.

Granted, a life of disciplined service does not sound very liberating. How is it, then, that liberation belongs in a study of initiation? Surprisingly enough, an ineffable delight in life seems to accompany this dedicated responsibility. Zarathustra, after many trials and disappointments, finally seems to sing and dance the "Yes and Amen Song" at the end of part 3 as if he has just broken through to a new realm of existence. Here, he has challenged the paradigms and value systems of the world of his fathers and of his contemporaries and reached a blue sky of clarity about who he is and what he worships or does not worship. In the second stanza he expresses with image the feeling of transcending worn-out ideas erected in stone:

> If ever I sat jubilating where old gods lie buried, world-blessing, world-loving, beside the monuments of old world-slanders—for I love even churches and tombs of gods, once the sky gazes through their broken roofs with its pure eyes, and like grass and red poppies, I love to sit on broken churches. (Nietzsche 1968, 340–341)

Remembering that the last phase in the flow of psychic energy brings to life a transcendent function of consciousness places the process in closer affinity to liberation. A transcendent function of consciousness means a completely different perspective—a unique attitude—toward others, toward events, and toward oneself. Jung concludes his essay entitled "The Transcendent Function" with a simple statement: "It [the transcendent function] is a way of attaining *liberation* by one's own efforts and of finding the courage to be oneself" (Jung 1958, par. 193; italics added). His choice of the words *effort* and *courage* describe the very foundation of service in the capacity of one's essence, truth, or core self. Framing liberation in such a way contrasts sharply with Jung's response to Eastern ideas of liberation:

> To me there is no liberation *à tout prix.* I cannot be liberated from any thing that I do not possess, have not done or experienced. Real liberation becomes possible for me only when I have done all that I was able to do, when I have completely devoted myself to a thing and participated in it to the utmost. If I withdraw from participation, I am virtually amputating the corresponding part of my psyche. Naturally, there may be good reasons for my not immersing myself in a given experience. But then I am forced to confess my inability, and must know that I may have neglected to do something of vital importance. In this way I make amends for the lack of a positive act by the clear knowledge of my incompetence. (Jung 1961, 276–277)

One may notice a tension between "immersing myself in a given experience" and the popular notion of liberation, so that I am again challenged to support the title of this last chapter. While writing these pages a dream visited me that seems to offer an image of the quality of liberation evinced in a blueprint of initiation.

> *This place is ethereal. I feel like a channel between heaven and earth, serving both. In heaven there has been a conflict, and the gods have retreated from a certain area, leaving a void. On earth, the people are building a temple and constantly supplicating the gods for help. They do not know about the retreat and the void. I am supposed to encourage the people to keep building and keep praying. I must not divulge the secret that the Heavenly Powers are not available. The efforts and prayers of the people will heal the rift in heaven.*

Liberation, then, does not mean transcending one's incarnate self. It refers to the sense of upward, outward, or forward movement of psychic energy and the sense of relationship to symbol, which implies relationship to the instinctual as well as the spiritual, or the unconscious as well as consciousness. It does not mean emptiness and detachment, or flying around in an astral body, clairvoyance, or separating oneself from the toil of life, even though any one of these experiences may provide valuable insights and memorable, sacred contact with ultimate reality. Even a naïve reaction to the dream might recognize liberation as attending to sacred creative life, "doing all that I am able to do," keeping faith with the essential truth that moves one to build a temple or light a candle or dust the altar, even when the gods seem unavailable. When the gods remove themselves to remote regions, a spiritual crisis commences in the culture, and at the level of the individual, a neurosis ensues. The one(s) to whom we pray can no longer hear. *I Ching* hexagram twelve, *pĭ* (Obstruction), reflects this situation; Karcher explains that it means "the old that must be sacrificed, ... the victim, the shadow, the Old King, the demon, the thing that blocks and obstructs and must be offered up" (2003, 144). The inquirer receives advice to "diminish involvement in the world . . . retreat and be patient" (ibid., 145). During my own retreat from involvement in the world I learned to develop a sacred attitude toward life. In solitude I have learned to move through my days with an attitude of faith, thankfulness, humor, and forgiveness (especially toward myself). Emotional survival during my retreat meant offering up layers of conditioning and habit and inner fictions so that I could hear what my only companion (the one who dwells within) had to say. I set to work building an inner temple, a place where the gods might find shelter should they decide to emerge from the hinterlands.

Reading over the dream after I had written it in my journal, the little word *retreat* captured my attention. Initiation means retreat, refuge, sanctuary, withdrawal, isolation. Is it possible, then, that the gods must initiate, to renew, develop, and individuate? Certainly the *image* of God transforms over time and perhaps the God-image in the culture is now in the throes of deconstruction and reconstruction into a more comprehensive form. However, my dream suggests a more personal form of retreat. Discourse regarding the person of God would serve no purpose here; however, I might ask, "Does the Self, Jung's term for one's individual indwelling of God, individuate?" Is devotional practice, such as prayer, vital in supporting the self through the conflicts in heaven or in the vicinities of the unconscious?

Western culture describes for itself an eternal, perfect, unchanging, impeccable, and complete God. The idea seems plausible and connects with a deep sense of validity in the ground of being. However, Job's experience with Yahweh suggested to Jung that God's wholeness remains unconscious; in other words that the all-powerful creator has an unknown capacity that calls it into a process that will enlarge and enhance all being. The calling arrives in the form of a challenge instigated by Satan, or Lucifer, the one who brings light through tricks and ruses. Satan's challenge causes Yahweh to behave unpredictably, resulting in a wavering loyalty toward Job, Yahweh's most devoted servant. My dream seems to offer a subtle but matter-of-fact assertion that gods may retreat, an act thought to bring insight, revelation, and unusual experience, resulting in a new perspective.

One might question the possibility of God attaining consciousness, considering the Western attitude that God reigns over creation with goodness and perfect benevolence. Jung explains that during the testing of Job, "Yahweh has become unsure of his own faithfulness" (Jung 1952a, par. 616). Yahweh eventually remembers Sophia, his feminine counterpart, and Jung attributes this turn of events to Yahweh's need for self-reflection spawned by his lack of self-assurance, a contemplation which requires wisdom, the essence of Sophia. Now the situation dons a complete motif of initiation.

Crisis proceeding from inner conflict engenders a need for separating oneself from outer influences, often imaged in shamanic initiation as withdrawal into the earth. Within venerated traditions of ancient cultures, mentored rites provided a stage whereby the archetype of initiation could constellate through imaginal visions and individual meanings could reveal themselves. Entering the cave within the earth or the imaginal space within the mind means entering a kind of womb, a protective space; it means retreating from the world of order and distinction and boundaries and contracts and complexity and slipping into a place of chaos where the part is not distinct from the whole, where images enacting mythic stories appear and disappear without announcement. Here in the containing vessel, the laws of physics no longer apply. Gravity may suddenly let go, bodies grow larger than large and smaller than small, animals offer help, and obstacles confronted magically open. In short, it is where paradox resides, and where paradox finds shelter, that wisdom emerges. *Lumen naturae*, light of nature, a term introduced by the alchemist and physician Paracelsus in the Middle Ages, describes the light of dreams, the light of imaginal space—an illumination concentrated on a certain act, often dim, sometimes interrupted by light that is blindingly bright. In a psychological sense *lumen naturae* means diffuse awareness, the intuitive consciousness that always remains partly unknown but allows reflection of one's essential truth. Such truth is often buried by fear, by needs, desires, and expectations hardwired into an ego that has long since forgotten its ally in the unconscious.

Jung concludes his analysis of Job's innocent influence on Yahweh's pondering with a provocative statement: "Whoever knows God has an effect on him" (1952a, par. 617). Here one finds the meaning of service as well as the message, perhaps, of my dream. Building the temple, an insurgence of the sacred into profane life, allows humanity to know God or to create a receptor that will channel divine energy so that relationship through communication may commence. This in turn stages a situation that encourages self-reflection, both on the part of the worshipper, as well as on God's part, hence initiation into expanded awareness. To continue the creative impulse through faith and tenacity and a simple appreciation of beauty consecrates humanity and presents a mirror for the creator. The "God, who also does *not* hear our prayers, wants to become man, and for that purpose has chosen . . . the creaturely man . . . to become the vessel for the continuing incarnation" (ibid., par. 746) and herein lies the bone-trembling call issued from distant spheres to humanity.

What does it mean in the twenty-first century, then, to channel divine impulse? It means first of all to have respect for life and then to celebrate it. Our human condition includes so much suffering that one easily forgets to appreciate and then enthusiastically embrace the immense beauty that permeates every moment. A person who has never felt understood by family will find it difficult to understand others or to live fully. This person may marry the "wrong" person or choose the "wrong" occupation or parent the "wrong" offspring or get involved with the "wrong" friends. Nothing seems right because the inner temple was never designed, never built, never decorated, never inhabited. This person's favorite haunt (whether it's the office, church, the gym, or a website or computer game) becomes the temple; life lacks meaning and always has for an astounding majority of individuals.

When one separates for a time from familiar life, the soul tends to blossom in unexpected ways. I know a woman in her fifties, grieving the loss of her mother who had died after an extended illness. Not knowing exactly why she must, the woman answered a call that took her to a small community in another state where she involved herself in various projects, both within the community and within herself. She encountered various inner figures through dreams and imaginal work which energized her for expressing herself in new ways. The experience presented many challenges, including a crisis that necessitated defending her own convictions. She could no longer perform within arbitrary rule structures that did not serve the best interest of others. Returning to her home and husband after several years of long-distance relationship, this woman knew a different existence. She had created her own space, developed her own avenues of participating in the community, and dedicated time to her artistic interests. She developed a perpetual relationship with life's mysteries and nature's ecstasy, even in its destructive aspects. She learned ritual rather than routine, silence rather than anxiety, creative expression rather than shopping, spas, and the superficial chatter of a circle of acquaintances. This woman found her way toward building the inner temple and now it permeates her every experience of life.

The shamanic tradition, no matter where in the world one chooses to study, can be traced back at least seventeen thousand years and suggests that just this enhanced awareness that invites the imaginal into conscious life indicates liberation. Since part of our psyches continues to live in the most ancient cultures, the internal initiation enacts a seemingly nonsensical play of images that do not connect with the external situations of modern culture. However, if an individual engages these images with the curiosity of a child and the discernment of a mature adult, the story unfolds to reflect the natural soul moving adamantly toward renewal, like the biological struggle of a serpent shedding its skin. Few modern individuals, unless their lives have "hit bottom" or completely unraveled, will separate themselves from the clutter of daily life in order to answer the call of a soul desperate for renewal. Consider this question: Does the serpent really *want* to enter the excruciating pain of tearing out of a skin grown too tight and brittle to protect and propel the long sleek body? Only humans, with well-developed and adapted egos, have the power to choose *against* nature's preservation of the organism.

What happens when the ego, with all of its avenues of resistance, decides to ignore, sidestep, or moralize against the soul's call to experience life in a new and different way? At best, one continues to suffer in meaningless, drugged desperation, feeling insecure, frightened, lonely, insignificant, and forgotten. Life seems like a bland continuum, occasionally interrupted by celebration lacking in spirit that at most gives opportunity for greater intoxication. Intoxication here includes anything that diverts one from the call of the soul. These activities often appear wholesome and right according to the value systems of a given culture. Included with typical substance abuse (legal as well as illegal) belongs over-indulgence in organized religion, exercise routines, friends and family, work, and therapies, to name a few. It is anything that captures one's attention away from the soul's work of shedding old familiarities and paradigms and renewing the individual and life itself. If grey malaise characterizes the best case, then what might describe the worst case? Instead of symbolic death of the ego through conscientious initiation, avoiding the soul's necessity leads at worst to mortal death of the incarnated life, most often preempted by prolonged disease. Disease results from many components; however, I have seen few adult cases of prolonged suffering with disease that didn't have something to do with a failure to attend wholeheartedly to the soul's journey of renewal.

Witnessing such a journey commands a sense of honor and ardent responsibility. The task requires perspicacious encouragement and perpetual self-analysis. In keeping with the foregoing dream, I must ask the question: Am I, not unlike Job in his faithfulness to the amoral Yahweh, to assure my clients that their God will support them just when it seems that they cannot go on? Shall I encourage them to keep "building the temple" even when they labor under the feeling that their prayers have gone unheard? Must I allow, for some unpredictable period of time until they are strong enough to withstand the psychic challenge of initiation, their fictions regarding a "good" God that takes away all suffering? I find that not only must I reassure my clients along these lines, I must open my own bones to the divine which supports and guides processes of renewal, no matter what form the individual process may assume. I for myself must take seriously these messages from the Self, the immanent particle of divine nature that pervades and sustains each individual personally, whether the messages come to soothe or to challenge. Inasmuch as building a temple, especially in terms of an inner project, parallels the alchemical process, a collaborative procedure of individuation, a purity of intention and moral strength (which operates under a different code than the moral codes of organized religions or society) enters into the equation, and I am brought back to the virtues of the adept quoted in chapter 2 (p. 40). In consonance with my dream, liberation also means prayer, meditation, and devotion. It means perpetual communication with the wisdom brought out of hiding, remembered and embraced during initiation. It means loving the highest entity of one's psyche even when it goes into retreat, like a lover who must go into seclusion to renew the heart that loves you. With reference to Job, Jung explains:

That higher and "complete" (τέλειος) man is begotten by the "unknown" father and born from Wisdom, and it is he who, in the figure of the puer aeternus—"vultu mutabilis albus et ater" ("Of changeful countenance, both white and black")—represents our totality, which transcends consciousness. (Jung 1952a, par. 742)

Transcendence most provocatively finds expression in the image of the feathered or plumed serpent. When the serpent becomes winged, nature and spirit have joined forces in order to further the spiritual development of human and God. Quetzalcoatl, the feathered serpent, occupies a prevalent position in mythologies of Mesoamerica. He symbolizes laughter and sexuality, expressive arts and domestic innovations; he essentially represents creative life itself. The majestic, green-plumed quetzal bird lends its elegant attire to the enigmatic, furtive, earthbound snake, lifting earth's wisdom from secret depths to soaring heights, from the most infantile instinct to the mystical complete person. The initiate experiences a visionary union of opposites that propels a renewed enthusiasm for embracing the challenges of existence, together with fertile ideas that lure one into varied dimensions of innovation, creating solutions that involve and benefit one's circle of influence.

Quetzalcoatl occupies a central position as a fertility god as well as god of creation itself. In Teotihuacán, Mexico, images of a feathered serpent—together with images of rain and water—appear on a temple building dating from the third century C.E. This was long before the Toltec (who thrived during the ninth to twelfth centuries) positioned Quetzalcoatl as deity of the morning and evening stars and the wind. The Aztecs, dominant in the fifteen century, elevated this enchanting figure to a central position as bringer of life and civilization. Later merging with Mayan populations, the Feathered Serpent took the name Kukulkan.

In an Aztec myth of redemption, Quetzalcoatl wanted to populate the world of the fifth sun, a world created after cosmic conflicts with his nemesis god, Tezcatlipoca. These hostilities created and destroyed four earlier suns and earths. Together with his twin, Xolotl, Quetzalcoatl descended to the underworld, known as Mictlan. Fleeing from the fury of the Death Lord, Quetzalcoatl dropped the bones he had gathered belonging to inhabitants of former worlds, breaking them to pieces. He managed to gather the pieces and carry them to Snake Woman, an earth goddess named Cihuacoatl, who ground the bone fragments into flour. Quetzalcoatl in turn moistened the flour with his own blood, bringing it to life. He and Xolotl shaped the mixture into human forms and taught them to reproduce.

This myth of destruction and renewal finds whimsical yet ideal embodiment in the Feathered Serpent, Quetzalcoatl, as prototype of initiation. One easily observes apprehension of a call to create a civilization under the fifth sun, and a negotiation of a crisis inherent in recovering lost life in the form of vitality and libido. This then necessitates descent to the underworld and a struggle with a death deity. Together with help from a benevolent deity who prepares a cure engendering life, there occurs an embodiment of liberation, which releases a newly created form to naturalize into a new genesis.

I said, O Love
I am frightened,
but it's not you.
Love said to me,
there is nothing that is not me.
Be silent.

—RUMI

Answering a call and proceeding through the tortuous passage toward a life lived with greater integrity, one may wonder just what essentials appear to remind seekers that they stroll (or crawl, or stumble) along the path to transformation. Remembering that call, crisis, and cure, each emphasized at different phases, all travel together, the most determined initiate may feel confused. Confusion arises when one is summoned to undertake the path of Tao, or Great Way. Recall that Jungian author Murray Stein adopted the term *liminality* to describe the central task of being in-between, in the throes of crisis. How does one discern between the confusions extant in daily life and the more tense spiritual confusion of initiatory trial? The latter moves one toward a goal that demands creative effort and sends meaningful apprehensions in the form of dream images or chance encounters that seemingly appear out of nowhere to point the way or offer wise encouraging words.

I am reminded of something my mother once said which I shall never forget and that I've never heard from another woman: "The pain of childbirth is not like any other pain because the enormity and excitement of bringing new life into the world are always with you." No stranger to pain, my mother birthed four children but also broke each of her legs at different times in her life. She emphatically drew the distinction between the pain of birthing and the pain of breaking a leg. Similarly, the confusion of initiatory ordeal carries within its struggle the sometimes oblique but always present awareness of birthing—in this case, birthing oneself. Birthing oneself means a delivery from attitudes imposed by family and societal milieus, from identification with wounds imposed by fate, and from situations gathered by the former, false self.

Contemplating Heidegger's words, "The calling is not a call that has gone by, but one that has gone out and as such is still calling and inviting; it calls even if it makes no sound," evokes the sense that we are constantly being called into life and into new life (1968, 124). During times of meaningful ordeal I return again and again to inspirational words that buoy me along. Sometimes the only thing that gives one a sense of forward movement is reading, or visiting museums, or attending performances. Sometimes it is reaching backward into the past and at the same time outward into the new for inspiration, guidance, and encouragement. Heidegger's words not only encourage me to accept the invitation over and again, they return me to the awareness of my call, singing its haunting chant no matter how far I may have wandered from the path. Wise words and validating images arrive regularly along our way, reminding us of the importance of our calling. Like helpers in a fairy tale, word and image serve as another indicator that we are moving in a creative direction.

For millennia the image of the serpent has carried a sense of mystery, embodying both poison and potion, death and rebirth, chaos and redemption. Not only does this archetypal image clearly embody our essential nature, it connects each of us with the entire history of culture, now thought to be at least forty-four thousand years old. For this reason, I draw upon the abiding characteristics of serpent to symbolize initiation in all of its aspects. In a poem by D. H. Lawrence, simply titled "Snake," fear, reluctance, and human pettiness overcome the observer, but in a moment of regret for interrupting his reverie with the snake by scaring it back into the rocks he utters the wisdom seemingly carried by the unaware snake: "And I wished he would come back, my snake. / For he seemed to me like a king, / Like a king in exile, uncrowned in the underworld, / Now due to be crowned again."[4]

Only a short time after I entered analysis a dream came to me which anticipated a transformation of the poison of the copperhead into a curing potion.

I am sitting in a room about the size of a small office, the floor writhing with relatively small copperheads. I have a needle and thread in one hand and a simple tailored white shirt in the other. I am calmly sewing the snakes into the collar of this shirt.

This dream foretells the goal of initiation: a cure that speaks a language only heard in the heart of its dreamer. The collar suggests authority somehow earned and bestowed, as in a clerical collar or the hood of a graduation gown. Sitting at the fifth chakra, collar envelopes a center said to contain the opposites of poison and nectar, a space of creative activity and devotion to spiritual practices. Meditation on this chakra brings one to the portal of liberation, and cure engenders liberation.

The serpent's bite in a dream or the bite of a snake in outer reality often means call. I am convinced that my four-year-old self received a call to destiny, even at that callow age. With no one to translate the meaning of such an inconvenient intrusion, I did not hear the summons until midlife when I came crawling to my dreams like a refugee of the spirit. Heidegger's words that the call continues forever always brought a soothing calm. Perhaps I still had a chance to take up my destiny and redeem my numerous regrets. The way forward is often frightening, even overwhelming, but the experience of enlarged possibility stirs courage and determination. Snakebite, then, seeks to impose on the conscious situation or attitude, to capture one's attention in order to reveal a particular something, an unknown, unconscious potential, or ailment, or blind spot.

Answering the call means beginning to prepare for something vague at best and totally unknown at worst. It means finding space, clearing space, or creating space and giving attention to the smallest or most undervalued thing. It means loading the vessel of outer life with only the necessities, discerning between the necessary and the superfluous. Daily life relinquishes its central position while one breaks away and into the imaginal. Like a shape-shifter, call arrives in many guises, in a score of voices, and at unpredictable intervals throughout the life span.

In the shedding of its skin, serpent embodies crisis: the struggle, the intense twisting, turning, rolling, tumbling, shrinking, and writhing. Like an innocent fool, I ran headstrong into the terror of myself, my solitude, and my longing. Reduced to the last thread of myself, I faced the necessity of weaving a new life. The outer world swam in surreal superficialities while love's mandate of silence deafened me with cries of loneliness and exile.

Serpent also images each component of crisis. It instinctively offers the old skin in sacrifice; its threatening fangs and long slender body have served as metaphor to describe a paradoxical passage and perilous journey. An imperative to remain devoted, like an alchemist carefully monitoring the flame, to stay the course, to keep the faith when all is lost, prevails. Inner and outer life seem to fade into one another, each offering challenges to expand expression and consider new definitions for describing one's identity. Yet, the mandate commands precise discernment, maintaining balance and perspective while one's very skeleton lies scattered in utter confusion.

Crisis announces the culmination of pain and the beginning of relief. Crisis means return to chaos. It means shedding skin, disemboweling, dismemberment, as well as the inception of birth, of re-membering, new skin, a cache of jewels at the very core of one's being.

When the symbol which defines one's life expression ushers a reconstructed body back into life, one emerges with a renewed sense of self-confidence, new ideas to order all activity, and replenished energy to manifest the ideations. Now cure permeates the atmosphere.

Cure means, essentially, a new attitude. It evokes Patti LaBelle almost exploding in the popular song "New Attitude." Cure does not mean once for all. It means a different lens through which one experiences the perplexing panoply of sorrow and joy inherent in life. Like D. H. Lawrence's snake, the exiled king of consciousness now venturing out to drink in a new life is often met with fear, lack of recognition, and pressure to act in ways habitual to the old self that the new self can hardly remember. Cure means standing in one's unique field of authority with a new dagger of discernment that perpetually carves out one's position in the world. It means constant refinement, constant relationship with imaginal wisdom, constant responsibility to develop and share the gift received, and constant devotion. Living one's cure brings liberation and affects others in expanding ways.

The image of Quetzalcoatl populating the fifth earth now provides a provocative image for what often seems like a yoking. Upon creating the fifth sun and earth, Quetzalcoatl did not sit down, tired and spent. The work of creation had to continue. He immediately ventured to the underworld to gather the bones of the inhabitants of the earlier worlds and fashioned new life from those bones, ground and moistened with his blood. Liberation in the image of feathered serpent means proceeding with the work of creation, expressed both through play and love.

Liberation does not mean escape from the suffering of life, or from struggling with the ambiguities always insisting on one position or another, but liberation from the insatiable yearning for material rewards and validation from the audience. It means recognizing the pillar that supports one's life and building a temple around it. Copperheads woven into the collar exact a continuing sacrifice and a continuing call, perpetuations of devotion to a life of meaning which comprise liberation.

The paths of transformation vary for each of us, but summon all of us with clear messages and inescapable imperatives. Dying takes many avenues and forms. The death required by individuation leads to new, longer, and more vibrant life, a life one deserves because one has paid the price. Flight from the summons, however, leads to another kind of death—a death of the soul which can only stage the diminished life. Every day, in sundry venues, we are each called to die so that we might live.

NOTES

1. In the temple of Asclepius at Epidaurus a particular type of harmless snake slithered around the floor where the supplicant slept. Any dreams or visions would be reported to a priest who would prescribe therapy by means of an interpretation. Wikipedia, "Asclepius," accessed January 21, 2014, at en. wikipedia.org/wiki/Asclepius.

2. An animated version of a talk on education given at the Royal Society for the encouragement of Arts (RSA) by Sir Ken Robinson can be accessed at http://www.youtube.com/watch?v=zDZFcDGpL4U.

3. Wikipedia, "Sophrosyne," accessed December 20, 2013, at en.wikipedia. org/wiki/Sophrosyne.

4. D. H. Lawrence, "Snake," accessed January 21, 2014, at www. poetryconnection.net/poets/D.H._Lawrence/834.

Bahn, Paul G., trans. 2003. *Chauvet Cave: The Art of Earliest Times*. Salt Lake City: University of Utah Press.

Barnhart, Robert K. 1995. *The Barnhart Concise Dictionary of Etymology: The Origins of American English Words*. New York: HarperCollins.

Campbell, Joseph. 1949/1968. *The Hero with a Thousand Faces*. 2nd edition. Princeton, NJ: Princeton University Press.

Castaneda, Carlos. 1993. *The Art of Dreaming*. New York: HarperCollins.

Cooper, J. C. 1978. *An Illustrated Encyclopedia of Traditional Symbols*. London: Thames and Hudson.

Doll, Mary Aswell. 2008. "Other Voices, Other Ruins: Beckett's Spectral Women." *Spring* 79: 125–137.

Eliade, Mircea. 1954. *The Myth of the Eternal Return or, Cosmos and History*. Princeton, NJ: Princeton University Press.

_____. 1958. *Rites and Symbols of Initiation: The Mysteries of Birth and Rebirth*. Woodstock, CT: Spring Publications.

_____. 1964. *Shamanism: Archaic Techniques of Ecstasy*. Translated by Willard R. Trask. Princeton, NJ: Princeton University Press.

_____. 1991. *Images and Symbols: Studies in Religious Symbolism*. Translated by Philip Mairet. Princeton, NJ: Princeton University Press.

Elkin, A. P. 1994. *Aboriginal Men of High Degree: Initiation and Sorcery in the World's Oldest Tradition*. Rochester, VT: Inner Traditions International.

Freke, Timothy. 2000. *Rumi Wisdom: Daily Teachings from the Great Sufi Master*. New York: Sterling Publishing Company.

Heidegger, Martin. 1968. *What Is Called Thinking?* Translated by J. Glenn Gray. New York: Harper and Row.

_____. 1984. *Nietzsche, Volume II: The Eternal Recurrence of the Same*. Translated by David Farrell Krell. San Francisco: Harper and Row.

_____. 2002. *The Essence of Truth*. Translated by Ted Sadler. New York: Continuum.

Hollis, James. 2009. *What Matters Most: Living a More Considered Life*. New York: Gotham Books.

Jung, C. G. 1932. "Psychotherapists or the Clergy." In *The Collected Works of C. G. Jung*, vol. 11. Princeton, NJ: Princeton University Press, 1958, 1969.

_____. 1934a. "Basic Postulates of Analytical Psychology." In *The Collected Works of C. G. Jung*, vol. 8. Princeton, NJ: Princeton University Press, 1960, 1969.

_____. 1934b. "The Soul and Death." In *The Collected Works of C. G. Jung*, vol. 8. Princeton, NJ: Princeton University Press, 1960, 1969.

_____. 1934c. "The Development of Personality." In *The Collected Works of C. G. Jung*, vol. 17. Princeton, NJ: Princeton University Press, 1954.

_____. 1935. "The Relations between the Ego and the Unconscious." In *The Collected Works of C. G. Jung*, vol. 7. Princeton, NJ: Princeton University Press, 1953, 1966.

_____. 1943. "On the Psychology of the Unconscious." In *The Collected Works of C. G. Jung*, vol. 7. Princeton, NJ: Princeton University Press, 1953, 1966.

_____. 1944. *Psychology and Alchemy*, vol. 12, *The Collected Works of C. G. Jung*. Princeton, NJ: Princeton University Press, 1953, 1968.

_____. 1946. "Psychology of the Transference." In *The Collected Works of C. G. Jung*, vol. 16. Princeton, NJ: Princeton University Press, 1954, 1966.

_____. 1948a. "On Psychic Energy." In *The Collected Works of C. G. Jung*, vol. 8. Princeton, NJ: Princeton University Press, 1960, 1969.

_____. 1948b. "On the Nature of Dreams." In *The Collected Works of C. G. Jung*, vol. 8. Princeton, NJ: Princeton University Press, 1960, 1969.

_____. 1948c. "The Psychological Foundations of Belief in Spirits." In *The Collected Works of C. G. Jung*, vol. 8. Princeton, NJ: Princeton University Press, 1960, 1969.

_____. 1951. "The Psychology of the Child Archetype." In *The Collected Works of C. G. Jung*, vol. 9i. Princeton, NJ: Princeton University Press, 1959, 1968.

_____. 1952a. "Answer to Job." In *The Collected Works of C. G. Jung*, vol. 11. Princeton, NJ: Princeton University Press, 1958, 1969.

_____. 1952b. *Symbols of Transformation*, vol. 5, *The Collected Works of C. G. Jung*. Princeton, NJ: Princeton University Press, 1956.

_____. 1952c. "Synchronicity: An Acausal Connecting Principle." In *The Collected Works of C. G. Jung*, vol. 8. Princeton, NJ: Princeton University Press, 1960, 1969.

_____. 1954a. "On the Nature of the Psyche." In *The Collected Works of C. G. Jung*, vol. 8. Princeton, NJ: Princeton University Press, 1960, 1969.

_____. 1954b. "On the Psychology of the Trickster-Figure." In *The Collected Works of C. G. Jung*, vol. 9i. Princeton, NJ: Princeton University Press, 1959, 1968.

_____. 1954c. "The Philosophical Tree." In *The Collected Works of C. G. Jung*, vol. 13. Princeton, NJ: Princeton University Press, 1967.

_____. 1955–56. *Mysterium Coniunctionis*, vol. 14, *The Collected Works of C.*

G. Jung. Princeton, NJ: Princeton University Press, 1963, 1970.

———. 1957. "Commentary on 'The Secret of the Golden Flower.'" In *The Collected Works of C. G. Jung*, vol. 13. Princeton, NJ: Princeton University Press, 1967.

———. 1958. "The Transcendent Function." In *The Collected Works of C. G. Jung*, vol. 8. Princeton, NJ: Princeton University Press, 1960, 1969.

———. 1961. *Memories, Dreams, Reflections*. Recorded and edited by Aniela Jaffé. Translated by Richard and Clara Winston. New York: Vintage Books, 1989.

———. 1989. *Analytical Psychology: Notes of the Seminar Given in 1925*. Edited by William McGuire. Princeton, NJ: Princeton University Press.

Karcher, Stephen. 2003. *Total I Ching: Myths for Change*. London: Time Warner Books.

Krishna, Gopi. 1997. *Kundalini: The Evolutionary Energy in Man*. Boston: Shambhala.

Lowenthal, Martin. 2004. *Alchemy of the Soul: The Eros and Psyche Myth as a Guide to Transformation*. Berwick, ME: Nicolas-Hays.

Luke, Helen M. 2000. *Such Stuff as Dreams Are Made On: The Autobiography and Journals of Helen M. Luke*. New York: Bell Tower.

Nietzsche, Friedrich. 1968. *The Portable Nietzsche*. Edited and translated by Walter Kaufmann. New York: Penguin.

Rilke, Rainer Maria. 1984. *Letters to a Young Poet*. Translated by Stephen Mitchell. New York: Vintage Books.

Rowling, J. K. 1997. *Harry Potter and the Sorcerer's Stone*. New York: Arthur A. Levine Books.

Rumi, Jelalludin. 1995. *The Essential Rumi*. Translated by Coleman Barks, with John Moyne. New York: HarperCollins.

Ryan, Robert E. 2002. *Shamanism and the Psychology of C. G. Jung: The Great Circle*. London: Vega.

Sannella, Lee. 1976. *Kundalini: Psychosis or Transcendence?* San Francisco: H. S. Dakin, 1981.

Sherwood, Dyane N. 2007. "The Traditional Plains Indian Vision Quest: Initiation and Individuation." In *Initiation: The Living Reality of an Archetype*, edited by Thomas Kirsch, Virginia Beane Rutter, and Thomas Singer, 103–122. New York: Routledge.

Stein, Murray. 1983. *In Midlife: A Jungian Perspective*. Putnam, CT: Spring Publications.

———. 2006. *The Principle of Individuation: Toward the Development of Human Consciousness*. Wilmette, IL: Chiron Publications.

———. 2007. "On Modern Initiation into the Spiritual: A Psychological View."

In *Initiation: The Living Reality of an Archetype*, edited by Thomas Kirsch, Virginia Beane Rutter, and Thomas Singer, 85–102. New York: Routledge.

Turner, Edith. 1996. "Reenactment of Traditional Rites of Passage." In *Crossroads: The Quest for Contemporary Rites of Passage*, edited by Louise Carus Mahdi, Nancy Geyer Christopher, and Michael Meade, 275–285. La Salle, IL: Open Court.

von Franz, Marie-Louise. 1998. *On Dreams and Death: A Jungian Perspective.* Translated by Emmanuel Kennedy-Xypolitas and Vernon Brooks. Chicago: Open Court.

Waters, Frank. 1963. *Book of the Hopi*. New York: Penguin Books.

Zimmer, Heinrich. 1946. *Myths and Symbols in Indian Art and Civilization.* Edited by Joseph Campbell. Princeton, NJ: Princeton University Press.

CPSIA information can be obtained at www.ICGtesting.com
Printed in the USA
BVOW04s0827161014

370869BV00001B/2/P